THE BARGAIN WITH AMERICA

I0425237

A Donald Trump Manifesto
and Integrity Judgment

Book 1 of "IN SPITE OF THEM"

Janvier T. Chando

TISI BOOKS
www.tisibooks.com

NEW YORK, RALEIGH, LONDON, AMSTERDAM

ISBN-13: 978-1-0884-0043-2
ISBN-10: 1-0884-0043-4

PUBLISHED BY TISI BOOKS
www.tisibooks.com

NEW YORK, RALEIGH, LONDON, AMSTERDAM

Printed in The United States of America

DEDICATION

This book is dedicated to those whose altruist missions in life wise up those considered the fools of the world.

ACKNOWLEDGEMENTS

My deepest, warmest and everlasting thanks to Salomon
Muna Yakana, Macdonald Chanda, Emos Mbiatom

Contents

THE BARGAIN WITH AMERICA

A Donald Trump Manifesto
and Integrity Judgment

Book 1 of "IN SPITE OF THEM"

Quotes

"The most dangerous man, to any government, is the man who is able to think things out for himself without regard to the prevailing superstitions and taboos. Almost inevitably he comes to the conclusion that the government he lives under is dishonest, insane and intolerable, and so, if he is romantic, he tries to change it. And even if he is not romantic personally he is apt to spread discontent among those who are."

H.L. Mencken

"The darkest places in hell are reserved for those who maintain their neutrality in times of moral crisis."

Dante Alighieri

"In the end, you're measured not by how much you undertake but by what you finally accomplish."

Donald Trump

"The ultimate measure of a man is not where he stands in moments of comfort and convenience, but where he stands at times of challenge and controversy."

Martin Luther King, Jr.

"Live as if you were to die tomorrow. Learn as if you were to live forever."

Mahatma Gandhi

"Everything we hear is an opinion, not a fact. Everything we see is a perspective, not the truth."

Marcus Aurelius

"I have never let my schooling interfere with my education."
Mark Twain

"...The world gets blessed every now and then with unique souls who though burdened by their invisible crosses, still have the extraordinary strength to forge ahead in life and give others a helping hand at the same time. Despite their tribulations, most of us think they are fine. Even when the weight of their crosses becomes unbearable, even when they proceed in a breathless manner, we still have a hard time understanding that they are drowning. In fact, we even condemn them for failing to sacrifice more..."
Janvier Chouteu-Chando, Disciples of Fortune

"It is not the person with a lot of money that is happy. It is the person with enough money that easily finds happiness."
Alexander Zakharchenko

"You educate a man; you educate a man. You educate a woman; you educate a generation."
Brigham Young

"If you want to make peace with your enemy, you have to work with your enemy. Then he becomes your partner."
Nelson Mandela

"We are in the process of creating what deserves to be called the idiot culture. Not an idiot sub-culture, which every society has bubbling beneath the surface and which can provide harmless fun; but the culture itself. For the first time, the weird and the stupid and the coarse are becoming our cultural norm, even our cultural ideal."
Carl Bernstein

"Remember, remember always, that all of us, and you and I especially, are descended from immigrants and revolutionists."

Franklin D. Roosevelt

"Never compete with someone who has nothing to lose."

Baltasar Gracian

"Mankind must put an end to war before war puts an end to mankind."

John F. Kennedy

"We find that at present the human race is divided into one wise man, nine knaves, and ninety fools out of every hundred. That is, by an optimistic observer. The nine knaves assemble themselves under the banner of the most knavish among them, and become 'politicians'; the wise man stands out, because he knows himself to be hopelessly outnumbered, and devotes himself to poetry, mathematics, or philosophy; while the ninety fools plod off under the banners of the nine villains, according to fancy, into the labyrinths of chicanery, malice and warfare. It is pleasant to have command, observes Sancho Panza, even over a flock of sheep, and that is why the politicians raise their banners. It is, moreover, the same thing for the sheep whatever the banner. If it is democracy, then the nine knaves will become members of parliament; if fascism, they will become party leaders; if communism, commissars. Nothing will be different, except the name. The fools will be still fools, the knaves still leaders, the results still exploitation. As for the wise man, his lot will be much the same under any ideology. Under democracy he will be encouraged to starve to death in a garret, under fascism he will be put in a concentration camp, under communism he will be liquidated."

T.H. White

"Here's to the crazy ones. The misfits. The rebels. The troublemakers. The round pegs in the square holes. The ones who see things differently. They're not fond of rules. And they have no respect for the status quo. You can quote them, disagree with them, glorify or vilify them. About the only thing you can't do is ignore them. Because they change things. They push the human race forward. And while some may see them as the crazy ones, we see genius. Because the people who are crazy enough to think they can change the world, are the ones who do."

Rob Siltanen

Maps

Map of the USA

2008 Presidential Election Map

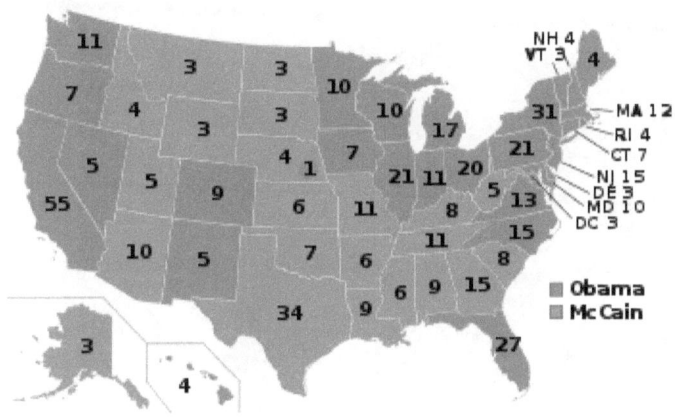

2012 Presidential Election Map

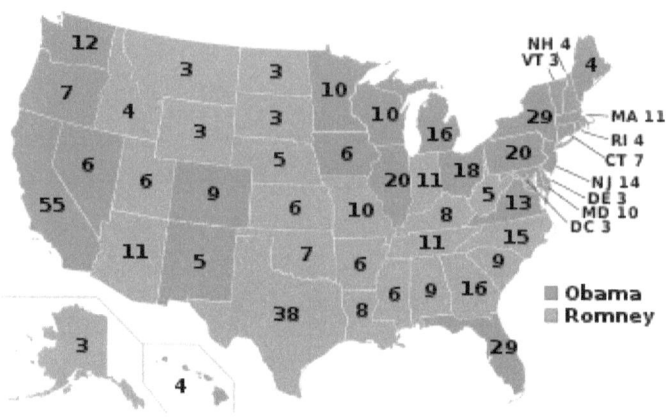

2016 Presidential Election Map

Democratic Party
Republican Party
Libertarian Party
Green Party
Constitution Party

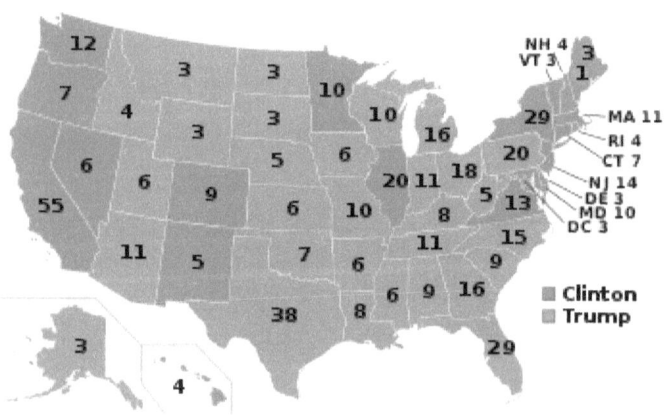

Summary of results of the 2004-2016 presidential elections

States carried by the Republicans in all four elections
States carried by the Republicans in three of the four elections
States carried by each party twice in the four elections
States carried by the Democrats in three of the four elections
States carried by the Democrats in all four elections

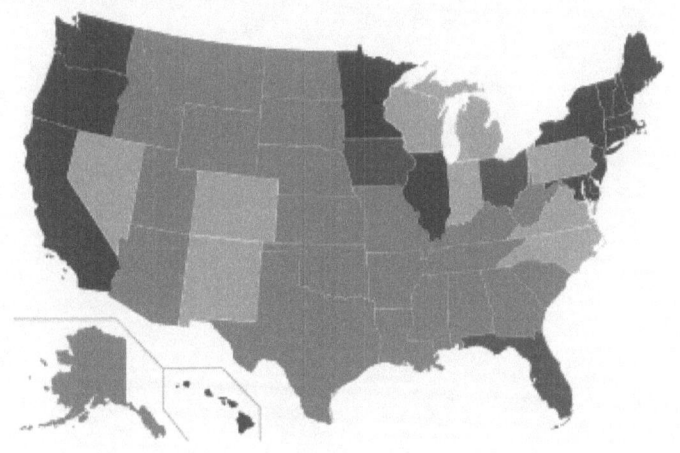

Prolegomenon

This account is not aimed at promoting or undermining the Trump presidency. It is as unbiased as any reader can get. It was a difficult book to write as I had to put aside my political inclination, social solidarity and cultural sympathy in the difficult task of presenting this analysis in a balanced manner devoid of stereotypes, unfettered by agendas and uninfluenced by propaganda. It involved months of exchanges with experts, academic research, talking with voters, and of discussions with people who have nothing to gain from the political developments in the country, but have a cryptic understanding of the developments in the country's political life. All of these gentle souls that mirror the American society contributed enormously in making this book a balanced account of the first thirty months of the Trump presidency.

The atypical nature of Donald Trump's presidency dominated the conversations of most families and friends that gathered together to break bread or to toast drinks at their homes, eateries, bars and other public places during the major holidays. However, if in 2016 and the better part of 2017, the topic of discussion was on how the businessman and television star won the 2016 presidential election, rattled the political establishment, mortified the mainstream media and awed if not stunned most Americans and the majority of the informed people of the world, the exchanges today have become more reflective, sober, grim and uncompromising, reflecting the polarizing nature of politics today, especially in the United States of America.

The current nature of politics in the country is a reflection of the apparent hardening of the opinions, beliefs, and positions of the two mainstream political parties, developments that the populations supporting them or their points of view tend to amplify.

Discussions, conversations, arguments, counsels and debates these days tend to be more about Donald J. Trump's logic-defying presidency — the inability to pin the 45th president down on the numerous claims or allegations made against him; the so-called increased polarization of American society at a time that he is winning more support from the country's racial minorities; the alienation of America's traditional allies abroad at a time that he is getting them more involved in the working and financing of NATO (North Atlantic Treaty Organization), which is the intergovernmental military alliance between 29 countries in North America and Europe; the United States of America's economic and trade wars not only with America's adversaries, but also with its allies and partners; the president's apparent penchant to pull the USA out of economic and military deals the superpower had made with other countries, especially when he judges that these treaties no longer serve America's interests, et cetera et cetera.

The task of a pundit trying to find rational answers to the

turmoil in the country's socio-economic and political life arising from the blind and calculated actions of both the Trump camp and those opposing his person and his politics, starts with understanding the promises the president made, especially after he clinched the Republican Party nomination, and then went on to pledge in a more vigorous manner during the election campaign to "Make America Great Again" by:

- Renegotiating the North American Free Trade Agreement (NAFTA) and Trans-Pacific Partnership (TPP), otherwise called the Trans-Pacific Partnership Agreement (TPPA) based on a conviction that if changes are made to the trade deals, it would benefit American workers and American businesses or by withdrawing the United States of America from those organizations, and as a consequence, alter the terms of globalization that America's previous presidents — Republicans and Democrats alike — consented to

- 'Bringing manufacturing (jobs) back to America, thereby reversing the trend of globalization that not only sucked financial and manufacturing capital out of United States of America but that also adversely affected American industries, and the American working class, especially its industrial workers. That negative trend began since President Bill Clinton initiated NAFTA in 1994. He even said that "My plan includes a pledge to restore manufacturing in the United States."

- Imposing tariffs on goods made in China and Mexico, as countermeasures against these countries for their violation of trade agreements or for their engagement in unfair trade practices against the specifications of Section 301 of the Trade Act of 1974. The intended result is to encourage domestic production and discourage the increasing transfer of US manufacturing jobs to those countries. Donald Trump said, "My plan includes a pledge to restore manufacturing in the United States." He elaborated further on this by promising to be tough on countries with a track record on currency manipulation. On this, he explicitly stated that "Any country that devalues their currency to take unfair advantage of the United States and all of its companies that can't compete, will face tariffs and taxes to stop the cheating."

- Renegotiating the Iran Nuclear Deal so that the United States of America would have greater control over the mechanisms put in place to prevent Iran from developing nuclear weapons and from continuing to demand significant economic concessions.

- Rolling back the Cuban Deal that the Obama administration struck with the Cuban regime of Raul Castro. Cuba was the United States of

America's No 1 enemy in the Western Hemisphere for close to six decades

- Not making changes to Social Security, which is what most American voters want anyway, even though many in the Republican Party leadership want otherwise
- Cutting taxes to encourage the setting up of new businesses and the expansion of old ones — far-reaching Tax Reforms per se that would benefit the United States of America and its citizens
- Placing a temporary ban on Muslims entering the United States of America by suspending immigration from certain terror-prone countries and demanding "extreme vetting", a promise otherwise called "Muslim Ban" by Trump detractors.
- Working out a rapprochement with Russia
- Reviewing America's burdensome military ties with its foreign allies, especially those in the North Atlantic Treaty Organization (NATO) alliance
- Wiping out ISIS in Syria and Iraq, leading America in winning the War on Terror and securing the control of oil in the Middle Eastern region
- 'Building a wall' along the entire US/Mexican border and making Mexico pay for it
- Repealing "Obamacare" and replacing it with a

market-based alternative

- Carrying out a host of other changes as well, including a ban on Lobbying, the deportation of illegal immigrants, the cancellation of federal funding to "sanctuary cities", the promotion of American energy self-sufficiency by lifting "the Obama-Clinton roadblocks and allowing vital energy infrastructure projects like the Keystone Pipeline to move forward", constitutional amendment to impose term limits on all members of Congress.", reverse Obama executive actions, deport criminal undocumented immigrants and cancel some visas, nominate a Supreme Court justice, promote School Choice and Expand Education, work out an improved Child Care Law, Cancel payments to U.N. climate change programs and use the money to fix America's water and environmental infrastructure."

- Et cetera.

The fact that Donald Trump's campaign rhetoric made him even more of an anti-establishment candidate than Bernie Sanders was, especially his pledge to "Drain the Swamp", meaning "Cleansing Washington DC of political insiders who are out of touch with ordinary Americans"; the fact that he sounded revolutionary during the campaign in a manner that made it look like he and Bernie Sanders had the same campaign platform; and the fact that he avoided clearly spelling out the revolutionary tools and methods he intended to use in fulfilling his campaign promises, made him come across as that "Expected One" who would set capitalism in right in the USA, and reduce if not eliminate the excesses of an American democracy that some anti-establishment pundits thought was being suffocated by corporate interests, career politicians, lobbyists and transnationalism in their agenda to make the world a "Global Village".

True Donald Trump and his campaign team got their inspiration from Ronald Reagan, the 40th President of the United States from 1981 to 1989, who in 1980 promised to "Drain the Swamp" of bureaucracy in Washington, and then went on to create the Grace Commission that identified $424 billion of wasteful government spending that could be cut. Congress would not act on the Grace Commission's recommendations, finding fault in the report's overestimation of potential savings and its categorization of necessary spending as waste, but the experience rattled the political circles in Washington to the point where it is still vividly remembered today. As a consequence, the elites of both the Republican Party and the Democratic Party viewed Donald Trump with trepidation if not apprehension after he promised to "Drain the Swamp". That among other things explains why many in the upper echelons of the Republican Party wished for his defeat in 2016.

However, Donald excelled in the presidential campaign. He wooed voters, skimped on policies, promised the heavens to America's disillusioned and won the 2016 race for the White House in an ingenious manner. But then, his victory raised many questions. Some were:

- How did Donald Trump win the 2016 presidential election?
- Is he going to implement his election promises?
- Is he going to sway the Republican Party into working with him to carry out the sweeping changes that would be a classic case of self-surgery, or is he going to mellow out and tailor his plans to suit the long-term agenda of the Republican Party and the purported unelected bureaucrats overseeing America's smooth functioning, especially the country's security and long-term vision?
- Is he going to experience a gridlock running the country due to the obstinacy of the Democratic Party, just like his predecessor Barack Obama encountered deadlock during his presidency while dealing with a Senate and House of Representatives dominated by members of the Republican Party who made it a mission to thwart all his initiatives in their bid to make him a one-term president?
- Is Donald Trump's "America First" agenda going to be accepted by the bureaucracy made up of cabinet departments, government corporations, independent agencies, and regulatory commissions — a bureaucracy that

sees the United States of America as the world's only military, economic and diplomatic superpower, and considers it its mission to ensure that the country continues leading the world?

- Is Donald Trump going to renege on his promises, work with Congress, the Bureaucracy and the Judiciary in carrying out piecemeal reforms to move the country forward without threatening the fabrics of the state and America's unique position in the world?

If those questions sounded tricky or seemed inconsequential to merit a profound response during the first months of 2017, they can no longer be dismissed today because the United States of America has changed profoundly during the past thirty months of the Trump presidency, following what many consider to be the most unconventional election in US. history that brought to power a maverick with a populist streak. As a matter of fact, Donald Trump's 2016 election victory altered America's trajectory in a big way.

While it is true that most political pundits, analysts in the media and even the common folk had viewed his election as a rebuff to the elites of both the Republican and Democratic parties who thrive by working hand in hand with the giant corporations, the corporate or mainstream media, and the financial institutions (Wall Street, the banks, the insurance companies and the Credit Card companies); it is ironic that Donald Trump, the poster child of this blunt rejection of the political establishment, built his business empire by navigating the very same political establishment before he got into politics by launching his bid for the White House. So it begged the question in January 2017 of whether he was going to keep the promises he made to his supporters or not.

At the start of his presidency, many people were puzzled as to how he would "Drain the Swamps", a task that entails clobbering those he had rubbed shoulders with as a businessman.

It is obvious today that Donald Trump began his presidency with a vague agenda to turn the political establishment upside down and a pledge to "Make America Great Again", promises that smack of Anarchism than Conservatism or any of the other shades of Right-wing Republican ideology that provided the guidelines to the administrations of previous Republican presidents in the formulation of their policies. And since the most that past Republican presidents did during their presidencies was right some of the shortcomings of the American system, a setup that for centuries proved to be the world's most progressive socio-economic/political system in the free world, many wondered how Donald Trump intended to "Drain the Swamp" without causing the system's collapse, a system that most agree, stands to retain its emulative role if properly harnessed and revamped.

Americans, especially Donald Trump's adversaries, had enough reasons in 2017 not to take the political novice seriously. After all, he had promised the most far-reaching transformation of America's socioeconomic and political fabrics without presenting a plan or a clearly-defined thought formulation or ideology that could be viewed in the light of that of the Democratic President Franklyn Delano Roosevelt, who served as the 32nd President of the United States from 1933 until his death in 1945, who is known as the father of the "New Deal". So, it was hard to imagine that America's politically inexperienced 45th president could be capable of carrying out the far-reaching changes he promised his supporters.

The first thirty months of the Trump presidency have so far been peculiar, especially with the media being abuzz with all sorts of stories about him or related to him. Underneath the media buzz are indications that things are not what they seem. In fact, when a Harvard University report on the media coverage of the 100 days of the Trump presidency came out in May 2017 pointing out that 93% of the stories about the 45th president of the United States of America were negative, it raised many questions than provided answers. When hardly a year after that, The Media Research Center, which is a politically conservative content analysis organization based in Reston, Virginia, came up with another study revealing that media coverage of the White House by the "Big Three" broadcast networks — ABC, CBS, and NBC — still remains 91 percent negative, it revealed an unprecedented if not worrying trend, lending credence to the president's claim that many of these giant media corporations were involved in fake news and that they had made bringing him down a part of their game plan. Such a point of view begs the question:

Why is the 45th president of the United States of America's approval rating not low despite the fact that Americans are being barraged every day with negative news about him and his administration?

As Donald Trump anchors himself in the second half of his first term in office and starts positioning himself for another term, developments will show that his command of the highest office of the land could be more beneficial for the country than expected, as the conflicting forces in America come to terms with the reality of his presidency and as he too adjusts to the reality of consensus in decision-making by seeking common grounds with the judiciary and the legislative branches of government. The outcome of these unavoidable compromises from both the Trump camp and the camp of those who are opposed to or are lukewarm about the Trump presidency, promises to make the next eighteen months and potentially the next six years very colorful indeed.

CHAPTER ONE

Genesis

"Two things are infinite: the universe and human stupidity; and I'm not sure about the universe."
Albert Einstein

"The best thing to give to your enemy is forgiveness; to an opponent, tolerance; to a friend, your heart; to your child, a good example; to a father, deference; to your mother, conduct that will make her proud of you; to yourself, respect; to all others, charity."
Benjamin Franklin

"The enemy is not the one who is facing you with a sword in hand, that's the opponent. The enemy is the one behind you with a knife at your back."
Thomas Sankara

Just before the 2016 US. Presidential election, Chanel 4, a British public-service television broadcaster, interviewed the Slovenian Slavoj Zizek, and asked him if he would vote for Donald Trump were he a US citizen. Now, Slavoj Zizek is considered by many as the most prominent Marxist philosopher alive. So the interviewer was expecting him to come up with a response castigating Donald Trump and a reason for his harsh verbal reprimand that would have confirmed him in the eyes of leftists and the rest of the world as someone diametrically opposed to the Right-wing views and policies of the real estate mogul. However, the Slovenian and former Yugoslav patriot astonished his audience by making it known in very plain language that Donald Trump rightfully horrified him, but that as a sort of a bright side, handing the keys to the Oval Office and the nuclear codes to Donald Trump would "trigger a big awakening in American politics".

Donald Trump's victory was a rude awakening to most Americans all right. But he won fair and square.

- Some of the people vehemently opposed to the 45th president of the United States of America asked and continue to question how he could have won fair and square when he lost the popular vote?

- *He won the Electoral College by raking up more electoral votes, and in the peculiar democracy that is the United States of America's, the Electoral College counts more than the popular vote.*

- Skeptics and cynics of the 45th president of the United States of America's still hold that he was aided in his victory by the Russians and by the oversight of the then Director of the Federal Bureau of Investigation (FBI) James Comey when he presented his October 28, 2016 letter to Congress less than two weeks to the election day, stating that the FBI learned of the existence of emails that appeared to be pertinent to the investigation of former Secretary of State Hillary Clinton's email server and that the FBI would take steps to allow investigators to review those emails "to determine whether they contain classified information as well as to assess their importance to our investigation".

- *There hasn't been any proof of Russian meddling in the 2016 presidential election for the purpose of aiding Donald Trump, and it is hard to conclude that James Comey's letter made any difference or helped Donald Trump win the 2016 presidential election. One thing for sure is that Russian deputy foreign minister, Sergei Ryabkov, saw no reason why Russia should be suspected when he said during an interview with the Russian state media that "'quite a few' people from Donald Trump's* 'entourage' have "been staying in touch with Russian representatives.", *indicating that it has been the standard with all incoming administrations from both countries to get in touch and establish the basis for healthier relations.*

When we look back at the turbulent first months of the Trump presidency, we can only conclude that his electoral victory deeply rattled the political establishment made up of the elites of both the Democratic and Republican parties, the two parties that US dissidents like to describe as two sides of the same coin involved in a charade that gives Americans the impression that they are making democratic choices during elections. However, it mortified anti-Trump voters the most, spurring protest in the streets with them calling for the cancellation of the votes, for Donald Trump's impeachment. In fact, they came up with all sorts of allegations against him, including treason. But above all, Donald Trump's victory shocked the mainstream media who ended up making his name the most talked about in the history of US. presidents during their tenure in office. However, one thing that is not much talked about is how the Trump presidency is going to transform both the Republican and Democratic parties, and perhaps the American political landscape, which could make it possible for credible alternate right and alternate left political parties to emerge and challenge the two mainstream parties that have been shaping the history of the United States of America over the past two centuries.

A mantra I picked up from my good friend and journalist Franklin S. Bayen is that *"insisting on a fact that is obvious for all to see, hear and understand is a waste of time and resources"*. So, there is no reason to delve deeper into why and how Donald Trump won the 2016 presidential election against all the odds. Such an account would be voluminous. And that, of course, is not our focus with this piece. Donald Trump's victory was colorful all right. After all, his path to the White House was certainly strewn with casualties from:

- His overriding dominance of the Republican Presidential primaries in a process that saw him outperforming his rivals and running down other Republican heavyweights who tried to undermine his chances of winning, such as John McCain, Mitt Romney, Jeb Bush, Ted Cruz and a host of others
- The convincing Electoral College victory over Hillary Clinton after a gruesome presidential election campaign that was replete with nasty, shocking and unbelievable accusations levied by both candidates against one another
- The allegations that Donald Trump is a puppet of the president of the Russian Federation Vladimir Putin and an agent of the Kremlin whose promise to improve ties with Russia holds nothing good for the United States, the Western military alliance—NATO, the case for democracy in the world and the fight against terrorism
- Efforts to make the new president accountable for

allegations or claims of sexual misconduct over the years against a host of women he crossed paths with in his colorful social and private life before assuming public office

- Efforts to find fault in his past financial and business dealings, especially the claims of tax evasion that is further aggravated by his refusal to release his past tax returns.

However, to get to why the Trump presidency promises to surprise both his admirers and detractors, we need to delve a little bit into why he won the 2016 US. Presidential Election when all the odds were stacked against him. In short, we need to know why the famous "Reagan Democrats"—white, working-class voters who traditionally vote Democrat but who every now and then accommodate special non-Democratic Party candidates like Ronald Reagan—voted for the businessman and media celebrity in the 2016 presidential election. The reasons for his electoral upset that are presented here are sketchy all right, but the insight into the factors he tapped successfully to become the 45th president of the United States of America cannot be lost. In short, this summary is meant to serve as pointers in our journey to unveil the peculiar nature of the Trump presidency that will serve as the springboard to another Trump victory in the 2020 presidential election:

1. Electoral College/Popular Vote Disconnect: Before Donald Trump was declared the winner in the 2016 presidential race for the White House after

garnering more Electoral Votes than his Democratic Party rival Hillary Clinton who actually won the popular vote by a difference of more than three million voters, few people believed he would be victorious in such a decisive manner. It has happened only four times in the history of the United States of America that a candidate won the Popular Vote and lost the Electoral College. These were in 1824 to John Quincy Adams, in 1876 to Samuel J. Tilden, in 1888 to Grover Cleveland, and in 2000 to Albert Gore, Jr. The curious thing about this travesty of popular democracy is the fact that the victims of the Electoral College twists have always been Democratic Party nominees, which explains why more than 70% of Democrats and Hillary Clinton supporters consider the Electoral College process unfair and wish to see it reformed or abolished altogether. This is an upswing from 66% based on a 2013 Gallup poll. In fact, back then, in 2013, most Americans, irrespective of the political parties they were affiliated to, supported doing away with the Electoral College. The Electoral College and Popular Vote disconnect emanate from the simple fact that the proportion of the population to the Electoral Vote among the more populous states is higher than for smaller states. For example, as of July 2014, California with a population of 38,802,500 (12.18% of the total population of the USA), has 55 Electoral Votes (a share of 10.22% of the Total Electoral Vote), giving it a ratio of 1 Electoral Vote per 691,662 inhabitants. Meanwhile, Wyoming, which is the smallest state in the United States of America population-wise, counts 584,153 souls within its borders (0.18% of the total US. Population), and boasts of 3 Electoral Votes (0.56% of the Total Electoral Votes), giving it a ratio of 192,137 people per Electoral Vote. This discrepancy abounds in favor of several other states with relatively small populations. Trump focused on those small states too, which he called "States that mattered", so that even though he lost in populous states like California and New York, and as a consequence lost the popular vote, his win in many "Wyoming-like" states did the job of amassing him enough Electoral Votes to win the election. Today, doing away with the Electoral College is gaining more and more traction as evidenced by a 2018 opinion poll carried out by PEW on the idea of "amending the Constitution..." so that the President is elected by the popular vote, rather than through the Electoral College. 55% of those polled wanted a change to the popular vote, compared to 41% of the respondents who indicated a preference for the current system. A similar poll carried out months later by Public Religion Research Institute found out that 65% of Americans support the idea that presidential elections be determined by the national popular vote, as opposed to 32% of Americans who still prefer the Electoral College as the decider.

2. <u>Economy and Declining Income:</u> Donald Trump paid more attention to the Rust Belt states of Wisconsin, Michigan, Illinois, Indiana, Pennsylvania, New York, West Virginia and Ohio (an area which begins in the state of New York and stretches westward through Pennsylvania, West Virginia, Ohio, Indiana, the Lower Peninsula of Michigan, and ending in northern Illinois, eastern Iowa, and southeastern Wisconsin) than Hillary Clinton did in the 2016 Presidential Campaigns. As a matter of fact, most of those states voted Democratic candidates in the past. He outspent and out-campaigned Hillary Clinton in these former industrial states or industrial heartland of America where deindustrialization has been hitting the population very hard more than anywhere else in the country. His promise to bring manufacturing jobs back to these states that started experiencing a decline in their industry around 1980, brought back hopes of revived fortunes and good times. That is why the above-mentioned states provided him with the votes that made his Electoral College victory a landslide.

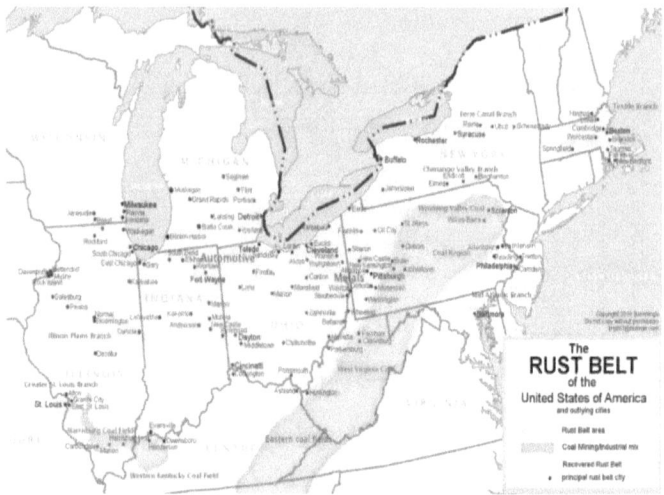

3. <u>Globalization (Jobs Moved Overseas):</u> Taken from the previous sentence above, we see that states of the Rust Belt were the hardest hit by globalization and the transfer of manufacturing jobs abroad to low-cost countries such as China, Mexico, and India. And since Hillary Clinton's husband Bill Clinton—the 42nd president of the USA, is credited as being the president who did the most in promoting globalization, NAFTA (North American Free Trade Agreement) and GATT (General Agreement on Trade and Tariffs), most voters in areas suffering from deindustrialization held the Clintons responsible, while upholding Donald Trump as the man who would bring their jobs back and "Make America Great Again".

4. <u>Immigration:</u> "Immigrants" in the United States of America are people residing in the USA who

happen not to have been born-U.S. citizens. It is a population that includes naturalized citizens, lawful permanent residents, legal non-immigrants (including those in the country on a student, a work, or other temporary visas), persons residing in the United States without authorization (illegal immigrants), refugees and asylees. Donald Trump's pledge to "take our country back", went a long way in allaying fears or in calming down the nerves of jittery voters, especially White Males who are concerned that the country is being overwhelmed by immigrants and are convinced that most of these immigrants are illegal, that the majority of these newcomers hail from Latin American countries, and that they took advantage of the porousness of the Mexican/American border by slipping through it virtually unimpeded by American migration authorities. His promise to build a wall along the US/Mexican border and at the same time make Mexico pay for it, though difficult to realize, made him come across to voters as a candidate to be taken seriously when it comes to the issue of fixing what is perceived by many people as a 'broken immigration system". Presented below by the Migration Policy Institute (MPI) of the United States Census Bureau is a tabulation of immigrant numbers and the percentages, covering a period of more than sixteen decades or 166 years.

Immigrant Numbers and as a Percentage of the U.S. Population, 1850 to 2016

Year	Number of Immigrants	Immigrants as a Percentage of the U.S. Population (%)
1850	2,244,600	9.7
1860	4,138,700	13.2
1870	5,567,200	14.4
1880	6,679,900	13.3
1890	9,249,500	14.8
1900	10,341,300	13.6
1910	13,515,900	14.7
1920	13,920,700	13.2
1930	14,204,100	11.6
1940	11,594,900	8.8
1950	10,347,400	6.9
1960	9,738,100	5.4
1970	9,619,300	4.7
1980	14,079,900	6.2
1990	19,767,300	7.9
2000	31,107,900	11.1
2010	39,955,900	12.9
2011	40,377,900	13.0
2012	40,824,700	13.0
2013	41,348,100	13.1
2014	42,391,800	13.3
2015	43,290,400	13.5
2016	43,739,300	13.5

5.   <u>Dissatisfaction with the Candidates</u>: It became

obvious way back in 2015, even before Donald Trump's victory in the Republican Primaries against candidates of the establishment such as Jeb Bush and John Kasich, and even prior to Hillary Clinton's close call against Bernie Sanders in the Democratic Party, that the 2016 presidential election would be a referendum on the ruling class in Washington, D.C. So, when Donald Trump and Hillary Clinton faced off in a campaign short on policies, it became apparent in no time that none of the other socio-economic and racial issues of the day mattered that much. Voters focused on the system, which they considered corrupt. Most of these voters also perceived Hillary Clinton as an integral part of the political apparatus or a product of the political establishment. Curiously enough, the majority of these same voters regarded Donald Trump as an outsider and political novice whose promise to fix the "degenerating system" resonated with them. That was why even though some Hillary Clinton supporters blame FBI Director James Comey for his decision to revive the Clinton email investigation barely two weeks before Election Day by sending a letter to Congress stating his intention in that regard, the Democratic Party nominee proved in many ways to be a difficult candidate to sell to those voters that deplore politicians they perceive as having a sense of entitlement and the conviction that they can act with impunity. These views held against Hillary Clinton were compounded by the actions of WikiLeaks, the DNC scandal and other related infamies.

6. <u>Clearness of the Message and Campaign Slogan:</u> Clear messages and campaign slogans that the Donald Trump camp came up with such as "Make America Great Again", "Clear the Swamps", and a host of others attracted a new poll of voters than Hillary Clinton's supposedly uninspiring messages and pledge to carry on with Barack Obama's legacy, which was a promise of continuity that failed to win over a substantial proportion of new voters. True, accusations of racism, sexism, and xenophobia tainted the Trump campaign and his candidacy. But even so, most Americans failed to find any inherent malice in the words and actions of Donald Trump that public scrutiny could use to damn him. Instead, as the mainstream media backing Hillary Clinton tried incessantly to tag Donald Trump with these prejudices or acts of discrimination, the political Right in America and most Trump supporters became convinced that the Left was carrying on with another "ideology of shame" against them. This explains even further why more blacks, Hispanics, Asians, and white males voted for Donald Trump than they did for Mitt Romney in the 2012 Presidential Election that he lost against Barack Obama, who at the time was the incumbent and 44th president of the United States of America.

7. Turnout: With a 55.3% voter turnout, the 2016 presidential election surpassed the 2012 race for the White House between Barack Obama and Mitt Romney which had a 54.9% turnout rate. And while this increase was up nationwide by 0.4%, it was higher in most of the states of the Rust Belt. Overall, 19 states experienced lower turnout rates in 2016 compared to 2012, defying presidential-year voting that tends to increase on each cycle that an incumbent is not participating in the Presidential election. Of note are Wisconsin and Ohio, states where a 3% and a 4% drop respectively in turnout rate compared with 2012 revealed upon analysis that it was mostly Democratic Voters who stayed away from the polling stations. And of course, these were mostly voters who cast their ballots for Barack Obama in the 2008 and 2012 Presidential Elections.

8. Rural Voters: The fact that the rural population is the fastest aging also explains why rural voters made up only 17 percent of the electorate in the 2016 race for the White House. Yet, this shrinking population that is reliably Republican and which the Clinton campaign thought it really didn't need, had an outsized impact in contributing to Donald's Trump's sweep of crucial Rust Belt swing states, where among other things, turnout in suburban and urban America was lackluster for Hillary Clinton. The Clinton campaign may have had some good

reasons for thinking that they didn't really need rural voters, a shrinking population per se that is reliably Republican. Unlike the 2008 and 2012 Obama campaigns, the Clinton campaign not only failed to win a rural council, but it also fell short of what it takes to come up with a robust rural-dedicated campaign infrastructure. Yet it had elaborate plans for rural America. That is why when the results trickled in on Election Day, the Clinton team that had what was on paper clear policy plans, found out that it had lost to a Trump campaign that made it a point of making stops in small towns where they appealed to these common folks "culturally". Besides, these rural voters never forgave Hillary Clinton for referring to most of them as "Basket of Deplorables".

9. <u>The Size of the Campaign Area</u>: The expansion in the campaign area in the 2016 presidential election was undertaken mostly by the Trump campaign team, especially in the states of the Rust Belt, most of which had voted for Democratic presidential candidates in the past.

10. <u>Education</u>: Hillary Clinton could have been thinking about the low level of education and low IQ of some of the people supporting Donald Trump when she described her billionaire rival's supporters during the campaigns as "…Deplorables". Of course, it backfired as those who thought she

directed that adjective at them mobilized and mounted a robust campaign against her in a way never imagined before, especially in the Rust Belt.

Demographic	Sex		Educational attainment			
	Male	Female	High school or less	Some College	College Graduate	Postgraduate
Trump	53%	41%	51%	52%	45%	37%
Clinton	42%	54%	45%	43%	49%	58%

The information above provides more insight into the level of education of the population and the choices made by the voters in the 2016 presidential election.

11. Democratic Nominee and the Media: There are many Americans today who are still convinced that the Democratic Party tipped the scales in favor of Hillary Clinton in the primaries, thereby denying Bernie Sanders, whom many considered a better challenger to Donald Trump, the chance to represent the party of Franklin Roosevelt and lead it to victory against Donald Trump in the 2016

presidential election. Most Americans also agree, especially after the casting of votes, that the blatant anti-Trump position that the elite mainstream media took before and after the election, and their blind support for Hillary Clinton, worked in Trump's favor as voters became immune to their negative news on him. The social media also played an underrated role in the election as a rising unorthodox information outlet that worked tremendously in Donald Trump's favor. The real estate mogul and media-savvy socialite's use of social networks gave him access to millions of people. What paid off the most was his effective use of Twitter, especially, as this social media network made it possible for his words to reach his followers in an instant, words that got retweeted to millions of others not following him. This use of Twitter, combined with Facebook's impartiality, helped to carry his message across to a wider audience than he initially envisaged. As the result turned out to be, the Trump campaign ended up growing the Republican base while Hillary Clinton galvanized her supporters without doing much to win new militants, supporters or even sympathizers for the Democratic Party. Actually, despite Hillary Clinton's outreach during her campaign rallies where celebrities and or pop stars like Beyoncé and Jay-Z appeared and even performed in support of her, and despite the fact that those campaign rallies were full of substance, those extra efforts did little to offset Trump's special focus on America's hurting working class. Something else that must not be downplayed was the fact that Donald Trump effectively tapped his name ID, media savviness and celebrity status.

12. Religion: Donald Trump won most of the Christian votes made up mostly of working-class voters and voters without college degrees because he appealed to their religious sensibilities, to their conservative values regarding topics such as gun rights, marriage, liberty, sexuality, abortion, and justice. Hillary Clinton, on the contrary, appealed mostly to the educated class and those who are liberal in their views on religion or religious values and practices.

Candidates	Religion				
	Protestant	Catholic	Jewish	Other	Atheist
Trump	58%	52%	24%	29%	26%
Clinton	39%	45%	71%	62%	68%

13. Ethnicity: The fact that Donald Trump won in the Rust Belt which voted for Barack Obama in the 2008 and 2012 presidential elections is glaring proof that he did not win the election on a platform of race. Besides, he got more Latino, Black and Asian votes than Mitt Romney did when the former Governor of Massachusetts ran against Barack Obama in 2012. However, a close look reveals that ethnicity played a major role in Donald Trump's victory in these states as more White Americans of Celtic, Slavic and German/Germanic ancestry voted for Donald Trump than they voted for Republicans in previous presidential elections. And the fact that ethnic Germans dominate in the Rust Belt partly explains why he won there. After all, he is of German/Scottish-Celtic parents and two of the three women he married have Slavic roots.

14. Russia/Kremlin-baiting: The mainstream media and the political establishment raved so much about Russia and its president Vladimir Putin during the 2016 election campaigns that the average American had every reason to think that the United States of America and its NATO allies were facing an imminent attack from Russia or that Russia posed as an existential threat to the USA. But then information from other media sources and from unbiased analysts pointed to something else

altogether. So, the fact that Donald Trump was resolute in his position to fix US. relations with Russia and its president Vladimir Putin defied the narrative that the mainstream media and the political establishment were presenting to the public. The unintended consequence is that many Americans now have an idea of what the manufacture of consent by the elite media is all about, the manufacture of consent that they had been made to swallow in the past that led America to get involved in conflicts abroad with the resultant loss of American fighters. So, the Kremlin baiting failed to convince the average American, who happened to be those who were weary and wary of war, to become rabidly anti-Russia or anti-Putin. Instead, the Kremlin baiting pushed many of these skeptics and cynics to vote for Donald Trump in the 2016 presidential election that is considered by most Americans as a huge bombshell against the country's political establishment.

CHAPTER TWO

Reflection

"I am convinced that men hate each other because they fear each other. They fear each other because they don't know each other, and they don't know each other because they don't communicate with each other, and they don't communicate with each other because they are separated from each other"
Martin Luther King, Jr.

A lot has been said and written about "How Donald Trump worked his way", or as his detractors like to say, "How Donald Trump fooled his way" into the Oval Office. The reactions of individuals and the different groups who rooted for him, rooted against him or who have been indifferent about him, have been nuanced. In fact, most pundits agree that no presidential election in the history of the United

States of America stirred such a wide range of conflicting emotions as the election of the 45th president of the United States of America. In a way, Donald Trump reflects America's current character, which though much cherished by its citizens and the citizens of other countries of the world, is haunted by underlying disorders and poignant conditions. He reflects America's split personality that has been growing over the years, especially after the September 11, 2001 terrorist attack on the Twin Towers in New York and the "War on Terror", otherwise known as the "Global War on Terrorism", which the September 11 attacks triggered, leading to the US. invasion of Afghanistan and Iraq, as well as to the United States of America's embroilment in other related conflicts in the Middle East, Africa, and Ukraine.

However, the fact that a high number of elites in the Republican Party objected to having Donald Trump as their representative in the polls said a lot about his true political convictions, which hardly anyone can say for sure what it is. However, judging on the divergent views of the 62 million supporters who voted him to the White House, we can say that the hope, rage, and fear invoked by his messages struck a chord with the over-riding emotions of those who supported and still continue to support him — people with a nostalgia for a United States of America that has disappeared, a USA that has become less homogenous and more globalized, an American superpower that seems to be becoming less and less concerned about the working class from whose shoulders and from whose elbows the "Great America" of yesterday was built, a working-class which was mostly "White American" at the time that the USA was overwhelmingly the dominant economic power of the world. Some pundits and most of America's White working-class that we are talking about saw in Donald Trump's campaign slogan of "Make America Great Again" not only a promise of reviving the nation by making use of them, but also as a rebuke of the path taken by previous administrations that downplayed their importance in the country's standing in the world. In the eyes of this fraction among Trump supporters, his pledge to "Drain the Swamp", confirmed that besides being on the side of the working class, he was going to work with them in neutralizing the upper political and business classes that were responsible for their socio-economic losses.

Therefore, as we go about analyzing the achievements of the first thirty months of the Trump Administration, as we try to figure out whether he is on track or not in fulfilling his campaign promises, we need to reassess in a lucid and unequivocal manner the promises he made in a bid to convince his supporters that he would be the best person to lead the country as the 45th president of the United States of America. In fact, during debates, interviews, rallies and other exchanges with the media before the primaries, during the primaries and during the campaigns, Donald Trump promised the people many things.

Now, the 45th president of the United States of America sent out a brief tweet on December 05, 2018, which read "Working hard, thank you!", with a celebratory image of a clapping Donald Trump with a banner behind him featuring the words "PROMISES MADE; PROMISES KEPT," and an imposing Statement "50% APPROVAL RATING" etched above it. This was just days after the media was abuzz with speculations that the Mueller commission was about to convict Michael Flynn—an adviser to the Trump campaign and a member of the transition team who for about three weeks was the Trump administration's national security adviser. So if Donald Trump is getting such a positive approval rating from the Rasmussen "and other" polling companies despite all the negative reports from the mainstream media, it begs the question what he is doing right? When the maverick president stated afterward that his approval rating could have been hovering around 70% had the mainstream media not been bent on undermining his presidency and its achievements with "Fake News", one could not help but admit that there was a grain of truth in his statement

Trump's approval rating (per numbers he's tweeted)
Analysis by The Washington Post.

If Donald Trump is getting an approval rating of 50% and he thinks he deserves about 70%, we only have to see telltale signs of achievements that have been clouded. That in itself could mean one thing only: Donald Trump has been fulfilling his campaign promises. The next question then is:

Which campaign comprises has he actualized, which has he failed to realize, which is he incapable of achieving, which has he ignored, which does he plan to tackle later, and which did he never take seriously.

CHAPTER THREE

Promises

"We can easily forgive a child who is afraid of the dark; the real tragedy of life is when men are afraid of the light."

Plato

"Hold fast to dreams, for if dreams die, life is a broken-winged bird that cannot fly."

Langston Hughes

"Success is not final, failure is not fatal: it is the courage to continue that counts."

Winston S. Churchill

"You don't have to be a Communist to see that China has a lot to teach us in development. The fact that they have a different political system than ours has nothing to do with it."

Julius Nyerere

Just before Donald Trump's inauguration as president on January 20, 2017, and even during his early days in office, most Americans doubted he could convince the Republican Party to work with him in carrying out sweeping changes that is a classic case of self-surgery for the party on whose back he rode to victory in the 2016 presidential election. His skeptics and adversaries, in particular, talked about his abrasive and arrogant personality that could not be mellowed to allow him to tailor his plans to suit the long-term agenda of the party of Ronald Reagan and the purported unelected bureaucrats overseeing America's smooth functioning, its security, and its long-term vision. There were astute analysts among the doubters who were even dismissive of the fact that Donald Trump made his bones as a businessman, one of those rare breeds with the flair to make the crowd follow them in their agenda. These sophisticated adversaries of Donald Trump are not altogether surprised that he is waxing strong.

Unlike politicians who play to the gallery by working with the crowd along the direction the people are heading towards, the business mindset dwells more on what needs to be done and then getting the people to go along with the game plan. As an African American friend of mine brilliantly put it; recent American presidents who happened to be nothing more than politicians were the types that would wet their index fingers by sticking them in their mouths, taking them out and raising them in the air to determine the direction of the wind(the mood of the people), and then go along with the prevailing sentiments regarding what to do; meanwhile Donald Trump acts like a business executive who determines the short and long term objectives of his company, and then gets the people to achieve the goals, thereby alleviating their wellbeing in the process.

So, the fact that Donald Trump figured out right from the get-go that he needed a consensus with the upper echelons of the Republican Party in order to carry out the sweeping reforms his election promises demanded, and that he also needed the support of some members of Congress from the Democratic Party to make his presidency less tumultuous, says a lot more about his acumen as a businessman than about his skills as a politician. In fact, he fared worst in his approval rating during his first month in office than his three predecessors. This was against the backdrop of a long list of reforms he had promised the population he would carry out.

Trump has far less support than his recent predecessors
Approval ratings for presidents after 100 days in office

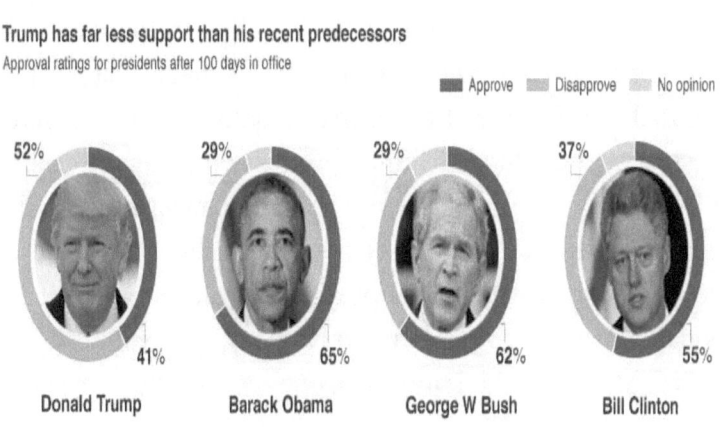

| | Approve | Disapprove | No opinion |

52%	29%	29%	37%
41%	65%	62%	55%
Donald Trump	Barack Obama	George W Bush	Bill Clinton

Source: Gallup (Data for each is from weekly average closest to 100-day mark)   BBC

Now, what does carrying out the reforms entail?

Simply, Trump supporters are not the only ones who expected him in 2017 and still expect him today to fulfill his campaign promises. Republican Party supporters, too, are not the only ones betting on working with him to realize the party's agenda. Americans, in general, are hoping that he would transform the bitterly divided United States of America into a country that is more prosperous, more stable, more humane, more flexible, less threatening, less threatened and that is at peace with itself and the rest of the world. The majority of Americans would love to see the America of their dreams realized within the next four or eight years, and most of them would care less if Donald Trump is the one at the steering wheel while that happens.

Realizing that ideal for most Americans during the four years of the Trump presidency would be like stretching credulity to the utmost. So for now, we shall dwell on the promises Donald Trump made to his supporters and determine the proportion of pledges he made that he has honored within the first thirty months of the Trump presidency, how those fulfilled promises tally against those still awaiting fulfillment, and what the chances are that the balance sheet would make or break him and his retinue in their quest to win the 2020 presidential election and make Donald Trump a two-term president. It would be a scorecard of Donald Trump's "Contract with the American Voter."

I: Renegotiate NAFTA and other Trade Agreements

Most seasoned American economists, public international lawyers, and diplomats were in unison and were even candid about it that a renegotiation of the North American Free Trade Agreement (NAFTA), the Trans-Pacific Partnership (TPP)—otherwise called the Trans-Pacific Partnership Agreement (TPPA), and other trade agreements or a US. withdrawal from these organizations are easier said than done because such moves would completely alter the trajectory of globalism and globalization that has been held sacred by past US administrations since the times of Ronald Reagan. However, Donald Trump pulled the United States of America out of the TPP on January 23, 2017, by signing an executive action barely days after his inauguration. Getting out of the barely 11-year-old TPP, a trade agreement between Australia, Brunei, Canada, Chile, Japan, Malaysia, Mexico, New Zealand, Peru, Singapore, the United States of America and Vietnam, was an easy thing to do since the agreement was not brought to the attention of the US. Senate for a vote during the tenure in office of Donald Trump's predecessor Barack Obama, even though the 44th president had supported it.

However, taking the United States out of NAFTA (North American Free Trade Agreement), the trading bloc comprising Canada, Mexico, and the USA, which Donald Trump had repeatedly described during his campaign trail as a trade deal that was bad for American workers, was expected to be a tricky thing to do. That is why when the president told the press in April 2017 that he had discussed renegotiating the trade agreement with the leaders of America's northern and southern neighbors at their request, there was a sigh of relief across the corporate world. In fact, he even tweeted that "Deal very possible!", meaning new dawn for NAFTA with the acquiescence of Canada and Mexico to his idea of a different type of trading bloc.

Even though more Americans (48%) thought NAFTA was not good for the country against 46% that thought it was bad for the United States of America, according to a February 2018 Gallup Poll; we see a bipartisan divide in the numbers. In fact, Republican support for NAFTA in 2017 was 34%, as against 71% among Democrats. So, it did not come as a surprise when the Trump administration announced on October 01, 2018 that Canada was about to join a pact it had already negotiated with Mexico. The resultant new trade agreement is the United States-Mexico-Canada Agreement (USMCA), which all three parties signed on November 30, 2018, at the G20 summit in Buenos Aires in Argentina. The onus is now on Congress to ratify the USMCA or revert to pre-NAFTA trading rules. Something peculiar about the USMCA is that it keeps tariff-free trade in most goods, which is considered the most vital feature in NAFTA. However, what it stands out over NAFTA are the improvements it brought such as:

- providing greater incentives for automobile manufacturers to produce their cars and trucks in the USA
- increasing environmental and labor regulations
- giving the United States of America greater access

to Canada's lucrative $19 billion dairy market
- the introduction of updated protection to intellectual property.
- encouraging online shopping and tech companies by raising duty-free shopping limits on goods entering Mexico and Canada to $100 and C$150 ($115) respectively without facing import duties, which are fairly above the $50 allowed before in Mexico and the C$20 Canada used to permit.

Some Trump critics hold that the USMCA is nothing other than NAFTA that has been repackaged, especially as Donald Trump failed to realize some of his initial demands such as tariffs on steel and aluminum suppliers, on big pharmaceutical companies, and on the automatic expiration clause. Still, it is hard to dismiss the fact that he came out of the USMCA deal as a remarkable negotiator who delivered on one of his core campaign promises, especially one that boosts his credentials as an American nationalist, if not a patriot whose love for the American people comes first, even above geostrategic concerns.

The whole idea of a unipolar world where the United States of America is the hegemon is built around the premises of free trade and international cooperation, with political and economic institutions supporting these regional and global economic and political relations. The overwhelming majority of these international institutions are led or dominated by the United States of America. This begs the question:

How far can Donald Trump go on the subject of reversing the globalization trend if he must fulfill his campaign promises to bring jobs back to the country, curb immigration, scale back on America's military spending and presence abroad, and defeat its enemies, especially the Islamist terrorists?

In essence, by using plain language and throwing in subtle words every now and then, the 45th president of the United States of America is asking the American people to buy American, a campaign he is leading by using the federal government, and by drawing from the "Buy American Act" of 1933 that requires the federal government to prefer US-made products over foreign manufactured goods. It becomes hard to imagine how the above-stated objectives can be accomplished in a world that saw the number of countries among the top 100 largest economic entities shrink from 36 in 2014 to 31 in 2016. This indicates a growing trend where big businesses or multi-national corporations have been growing their wealth faster than nation-states, a phenomenon that has increased their leverage and the ability to influence the domestic and foreign policies of governments in all the continents of the world.

Revenue of Top 100 Countries and Corporations in 2016

	Top 100 Countries/Corporations				
Country/Corporation	Revenue (US$, bns)	Country/Corporation	Revenue (US$, bns)	Country/Corporation	Revenue (US$, bns)
1 United States	3,251	35 Austria	189	69 Ping An Insurance	110
2 China	2,426	36 Samsung Electronics	177	70 United Arab Emirates	110
3 Germany	1,515	37 Turkey	175	71 Kroger	110
4 Japan	1,439	38 Glencore	170	72 Société Générale	108
5 France	1,253	39 Industrial & Commercial Bank of China	167	73 Amazon.com	107
6 United Kingdom	1,101	40 Daimler	166	74 China Mobile Communications	107
7 Italy	876	41 Denmark	162	75 SAIC Motor	107
8 Brazil	631	42 UnitedHealth Group	157	76 Walgreens Boots Alliance	103
9 Canada	585	43 CVS Health	153	77 HP	103
10 Walmart	482	44 EXOR Group	153	78 Assicurazioni Generali	103
11 Spain	474	45 General Motors	152	79 Cardinal Health	103
12 Australia	426	46 Ford Motor	150	80 BMW	102
13 Netherlands	337	47 China Construction Bank	148	81 Express Scripts Holding	102
14 State Grid	330	48 AT&T	147	82 Nissan Motor	102
15 China National Petroleum	299	49 Total	143	83 China Life Insurance	101
16 Sinopec Group	294	50 Argentina	143	84 J.P. Morgan Chase	101
17 Korea, South	291	51 Hon Hai Precision Industry	141	85 Gazprom	99
18 Royal Dutch Shell	272	52 General Electric	140	86 China Railway Engineering	99
19 Mexico	260	53 China State Construction Engineering	140	87 Petrobras	97
20 Sweden	251	54 AmerisourceBergen	136	88 Trafigura Group	97
21 Exxon Mobil	246	55 Agricultural Bank of China	133	89 Nippon Telegraph & Telephone	96
22 Volkswagen	237	56 Verizon	132	90 Boeing	96
23 Toyota Motor	237	57 Finland	131	91 China Railway Construction	96
24 India	236	58 Chevron	131	92 Microsoft	94
25 Apple	234	59 E.ON	129	93 Bank of America Corp.	93
26 Belgium	227	60 AXA	129	94 ENI	93
27 BP	226	61 Indonesia	123	95 Nestlé	92
28 Switzerland	222	62 Allianz	123	96 Wells Fargo	90
29 Norway	220	63 Bank of China	122	97 Portugal	90
30 Russia	216	64 Honda Motor	122	98 HSBC Holdings	89
31 Berkshire Hathaway	211	65 Japan Post Holdings	119	99 Home Depot	89
32 Venezuela	203	66 Costco	116	100 Citigroup	88
33 Saudi Arabia	193	67 BNP Paribas	112		
34 McKesson	192	68 Fannie Mae	110		

Wal-Mart, the largest of the multinationals that featured as No. 10 on the list above, and that raked in $482 billion as revenue in 2017 and $500 billion in 2018, amounts that are larger than the tax revenues of Spain, Australia, and the Netherlands put together, epitomizes the strength and influence of multinationals or global corporations. In fact, corporation wise, Wal-Mart is followed by China's electricity monopoly State Grid (No 14), China National Petroleum (No 15), Chinese oil firm Sinopec Group (No16), Royal Dutch Shell No 18), Exxon Mobil (No 21), Volkswagen (No 22), Toyota (No 23) and Apple (No 26). The combined revenue of these ten businesses is more than China's tax revenue, and it exceeds the tally of the bottom 180 countries of the world in a list that includes Argentina, Iran, Ireland, Israel, Indonesia, Greece, and South Africa.

Hardly anyone can deny the fact that many governments of the world have been bowing to pressure from multinational firms to promote business-friendly tax regimes above the needs of their own citizens, thereby eroding democracy in the process, since these big businesses or corporate juggernauts care more about their interests and profit margins than the democratic values of their different host countries, and since they have little or no qualms turning a blind eye to dictators that are "good for business". In fact, some of these giant multinationals back dictators, thereby putting their profit margins above the basic human values that these corrupt dictators and their kleptocratic regimes are stepping on or thrashing by oppressing their people. A case in point is the Frenchpuppet President Paul Biya of Cameroon (a rundown oil-rich and oil transit nation that hosts the United States of America's single-biggest investment in Africa—The Chad-Cameroon Pipeline that is anticipated to be extended to Niger Republic, thereby doubling its length), who has been in power since 1982 and who is noted for his chutzpah in staging elections that are massively rigged, charades per se where he does not even bother to campaign. These heavily flawed elections always get a pass from the puppet master France, big businesses (multi-national corporations) and other countries that also think he is good for business, since he has been granting them unfettered access to the country's resources in a process that is nothing more than a sell-off replete with every imaginable scam, all of which contribute in depriving the Cameroonian people and the public treasury of the benefits of the country's resources.

True the wealth and power of the giant multi-national corporations are at the heart of so many of the world's problems, ills that the USA has not been immune to and which Donald Trump promised to address. Even so, it is hard to imagine that the US. president would be able to reduce the influence of these giant corporations, the majority of which are American, giant corporations that are considered by some as juggernauts that are too big to fail. Furthermore, the fact that the United States has been leading the globalization effort makes it difficult for it to absolve itself of some if not most of the responsibilities for the problems caused by rapid globalization that has been poorly regulated. In short, this involves the process through which businesses or other organizations develop international influence or start operating on an international scale while exploiting the loopholes in international trade, international law, and the dark side of international control involving certain powerful individuals, groups and governments. As a consequence, the world is experiencing rapid growth in the number of pundits who think a unipolar approach towards resolving these problems would be futile. That is why the Trump administration needs to work with other regional and world bodies to come up with a binding treaty that provides a full range of rules, human rights values and responsibilities that these multinational businesses would have to abide by in their global outreach.

Also, when we take into consideration the fact that the series of World Trade Agreements signed by both Republican and Democratic governments over the years gave waivers to fifty-nine countries worldwide, which allows them to bid on contracts that most US companies are eligible to do, one cannot avoid but conclude that talks involving the renegotiation of past deals would entail a high level of diplomacy and a lot of craftsmanship. Renegotiating the terms of the World Trade Organization, in particular, would be cumbersome and lengthy, something Donald Trump has obviously realized. After all, didn't Democratic senators Tammy Baldwin and Jeff Merkley from Wisconsin and Oregon respectively get ignored after they wrote to the president in March 2017 demanding that he "suspends" the access that foreign firms have when it comes to making bids on US contracts such as the construction of the US/Mexican border fence, until the world trade agreement is renegotiated?

II: Create Jobs and Become the No 1 Job President

Donald Trump promised during the campaign to create 25 million jobs over 10 years and become "...the greatest jobs president that God ever created..." Realizing such a feat would put him above Bill Clinton who created 18.6 million jobs during his presidency (a 15.6 percent increase, which is the third-largest percentage increase behind Franklin D. Roosevelt at 21.5 percent and Ronald Reagan at 16.5 percent). Apparently, this is one promise he has been very fervent about realizing right from the beginning. As statistics from the table below show, he has been making quite an impressive headway.

However, realizing such an upswing coming mostly from secondary (manufacturing) and tertiary sectors entails convincing most American multinationals to dedicate some, if not most of their expansions in the USA, enticing others to bring their production back home to the United States of America, encouraging foreign manufacturers to invest in the United States, and promoting local small, medium and large businesses in the country.

Labor Market Information on States and their Unemployment Rates from 2016-2018 (Annual Average Rankings) as presented by the RI Department of Labor and Training:

State	2018 Rate	2018 Rank	2017 Rate	2017 Rank	2016 Rate	2016 Rank
United States	3.9	—	4.4	—	4.9	—
Alabama	3.9	26	4.4	29	5.8	44
Alaska	6.6	51	7.0	51	6.9	51
Arizona	4.8	45	4.9	40	5.4	39
Arkansas	3.7	23	3.7	15	4.0	14
California	4.2	37	4.8	39	5.5	42
Colorado	3.3	14	2.7	2	3.2	6
Connecticut	4.1	31	4.7	35	5.1	33
Delaware	3.8	25	4.5	31	4.5	20
District of Columbia	5.6	50	6.1	50	6.1	47
Florida	3.6	22	4.2	23	4.8	25
Georgia	3.9	26	4.7	35	5.4	39
Hawaii	2.4	1	2.4	1	3.0	2
Idaho	2.8	6	3.2	8	3.8	10
Illinois	4.3	39	4.9	40	5.8	44
Indiana	3.4	16	3.6	14	4.4	19
Iowa	2.5	2	3.1	7	3.6	9
Kansas	3.4	16	3.7	15	4.0	14
Kentucky	4.3	39	4.9	40	5.1	33
Louisiana	4.9	47	5.1	45	6.1	47
Maine	3.4	16	3.4	12	3.8	10
Maryland	3.9	26	4.3	26	4.5	20
Massachusetts	3.3	14	3.8	18	3.9	12
Michigan	4.1	31	4.6	33	5.0	29
Minnesota	2.9	8	3.4	12	3.9	12
Mississippi	4.8	45	5.1	45	5.8	44
Missouri	3.2	13	3.8	18	4.6	22
Montana	3.7	23	3.9	21	4.1	17
Nebraska	2.8	6	2.9	5	3.1	4

Nevada	4.6	43	5.1	45	5.7	43
New Hampshire	2.5	2	2.7	2	2.9	1
New Jersey	4.1	31	4.6	33	5.0	29
New Mexico	4.9	47	5.9	49	6.6	50
New York	4.1	31	4.7	35	4.9	28
North Carolina	3.9	26	4.5	31	5.1	33
North Dakota	2.6	4	2.7	2	3.1	4
Ohio	4.6	43	5.0	44	5.0	29
Oklahoma	3.4	16	4.2	23	4.8	25
Oregon	4.2	37	4.1	22	4.8	25
Pennsylvania	4.3	39	4.9	40	5.4	39
Rhode Island	**4.1**	**31**	**4.4**	**29**	**5.2**	**36**
South Carolina	3.4	16	4.3	26	5.0	29
South Dakota	3.0	9	3.2	8	3.0	2
Tennessee	3.5	21	3.8	18	4.7	24
Texas	3.9	26	4.3	26	4.6	22
Utah	3.1	12	3.3	10	3.4	8
Vermont	2.7	5	3.0	6	3.2	6
Virginia	3.0	9	3.7	15	4.1	17
Washington	4.5	42	4.7	35	5.3	37
West Virginia	5.3	49	5.2	48	6.1	47
Wisconsin	3.0	9	3.3	10	4.0	14
Wyoming	4.1	31	4.2	23	5.3	37

It is apparent that the 45th US. President has proven his mettle in this regard not only in discouraging manufacturers from relocating abroad but also in increasing manufacturing at home. Regarding dissuading American companies from setting up plants abroad, Ford Automobile stands out as a classic case in point. Donald Trump convinced America's No 2 automobile manufacturer not to establish new plants in Mexico, so that what we have today is the skeletal remains of the partially constructed Ford plant looming over the Mexican desert in the state of San Luis Potosi, instead of what should by now have been an operating plant churning out cars for the Mexican, Canadian and US. markets. It is now 800 plus days into the Trump presidency, so such development is counted as a victory in keeping his campaign promises.

In a nutshell, it is too early to determine whether the promise the president made in the 2016 primaries and campaigns to create more jobs, restore America's manufacturing capacity, and take the country to newer heights, would meet the expectations of his supporters and Americans in general. Here, he can surprise his skeptics by not only restoring America's manufacturing prowess and bringing jobs back to former manufacturing areas of the country, but by also overseeing a boom in new industries. However, he is on track in living up to this particular promise, based on the decrease in the rate of unemployment, and the increase in the number of jobs created over the years, especially in the manufacturing sector.

Unemployment Rate (%) for Americans 16 years old and over

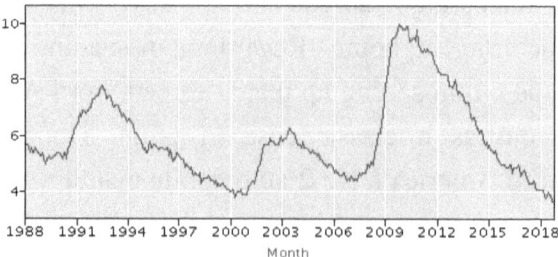

An analysis of the graph above and the table below presented by Brookings Institution, which is an American group that conducts research and education in the social sciences, reveals that there has been substantial growth in manufacturing jobs since Donald Trump's inauguration on January 20, 2018. The table below on the rate of unemployment over the years can be used as a matrix to confirm that finding.

Unemployment Rate (%) in the USA in the Last Three Decades

Year	Jan	Feb	Mar	Apr	May	Jun	Jul	Aug	Sep	Oct	Nov	Dec
1988	5.7	5.7	5.7	5.4	5.6	5.4	5.4	5.6	5.4	5.4	5.3	5.3
1989	5.4	5.2	5.0	5.2	5.2	5.3	5.2	5.2	5.3	5.3	5.4	5.4
1990	5.4	5.3	5.2	5.4	5.4	5.2	5.5	5.7	5.9	5.9	6.2	6.3
1991	6.4	6.6	6.8	6.7	6.9	6.9	6.8	6.9	6.9	7.0	7.0	7.3
1992	7.3	7.4	7.4	7.4	7.6	7.8	7.7	7.6	7.6	7.3	7.4	7.4
1993	7.3	7.1	7.0	7.1	7.1	7.0	6.9	6.8	6.7	6.8	6.6	6.5
1994	6.6	6.6	6.5	6.4	6.1	6.1	6.1	6.0	5.9	5.8	5.6	5.5
1995	5.6	5.4	5.4	5.8	5.6	5.6	5.7	5.7	5.6	5.5	5.6	5.6
1996	5.6	5.5	5.5	5.6	5.6	5.3	5.5	5.1	5.2	5.2	5.4	5.4
1997	5.3	5.2	5.2	5.1	4.9	5.0	4.9	4.8	4.9	4.7	4.6	4.7
1998	4.6	4.6	4.7	4.3	4.4	4.5	4.5	4.5	4.6	4.5	4.4	4.4
1999	4.3	4.4	4.2	4.3	4.2	4.3	4.3	4.2	4.2	4.1	4.1	4.0
2000	4.0	4.1	4.0	3.8	4.0	4.0	4.0	4.1	3.9	3.9	3.9	3.9
2001	4.2	4.2	4.3	4.4	4.3	4.5	4.6	4.9	5.0	5.3	5.5	5.7
2002	5.7	5.7	5.7	5.9	5.8	5.8	5.8	5.7	5.7	5.7	5.9	6.0
2003	5.8	5.9	5.9	6.0	6.1	6.3	6.2	6.1	6.1	6.0	5.8	5.7
2004	5.7	5.6	5.8	5.6	5.6	5.6	5.5	5.4	5.4	5.5	5.4	5.4
2005	5.3	5.4	5.2	5.2	5.1	5.0	5.0	4.9	5.0	5.0	5.0	4.9

Year	Jan	Feb	Mar	Apr	May	Jun	Jul	Aug	Sep	Oct	Nov	Dec
2006	4.7	4.8	4.7	4.7	4.6	4.6	4.7	4.7	4.5	4.4	4.5	4.4
2007	4.6	4.5	4.4	4.5	4.4	4.6	4.7	4.6	4.7	4.7	4.7	5.0
2008	5.0	4.9	5.1	5.0	5.4	5.6	5.8	6.1	6.1	6.5	6.8	7.3
2009	7.8	8.3	8.7	9.0	9.4	9.5	9.5	9.6	9.8	10.0	9.9	9.9
2010	9.8	9.8	9.9	9.9	9.6	9.4	9.4	9.5	9.5	9.4	9.8	9.3
2011	9.1	9.0	9.0	9.1	9.0	9.1	9.0	9.0	9.0	8.8	8.6	8.5
2012	8.3	8.3	8.2	8.2	8.2	8.2	8.2	8.1	7.8	7.8	7.7	7.9
2013	8.0	7.7	7.5	7.6	7.5	7.5	7.3	7.2	7.2	7.2	6.9	6.7
2014	6.6	6.7	6.7	6.3	6.3	6.1	6.2	6.2	5.9	5.7	5.8	5.6
2015	5.7	5.5	5.5	5.4	5.5	5.3	5.2	5.1	5.0	5.0	5.0	5.0
2016	4.9	4.9	5.0	5.0	4.7	4.9	4.9	4.9	5.0	4.9	4.6	4.7
2017	4.8	4.7	4.5	4.4	4.3	4.3	4.3	4.4	4.2	4.1	4.1	4.1
2018	4.1	4.1	4.1	3.9	3.8	4.0	3.9	3.9	3.7	3.7	3.7	

The change in the rate of unemployment over the decades and years as shown below is highly uneven, with some states registering higher improvements than others. Of particular note is the fact that the 2018 unemployment rate is the lowest in more than two decades, even though many skeptics and cynics who distrust the current methods employed in Labor Force Sample Surveys hold that these procedures favor current administrations than previous ones, especially in an era where small and medium-size businesses abound, and where the preponderance of sole proprietorships and other solo forms of making money mean that those who are able to survive on their own without working for someone, for a business or for a public entity such as the government are less likely to register themselves as unemployed.

States with unemployment rates significantly different from that of the U.S., February 2019, seasonally adjusted as presented by the Department of Labor's Bureau of Labor Statistics:

State	Rate(p)
United States (1)	3.8
Alaska	6.5
Arizona	5.1
California	4.2
District of Columbia	5.5
Hawaii	2.7
Idaho	2.9
Iowa	2.4
Louisiana	4.9
Massachusetts	3.0
Minnesota	3.1
Mississippi	4.8
Nebraska	2.8
New Hampshire	2.4
New Mexico	5.1
North Dakota	2.4
Ohio	4.6
Oklahoma	3.3
South Carolina	3.2
South Dakota	2.9
Tennessee	3.2
Utah	3.0
Vermont	2.4
Virginia	2.9
Washington	4.5
West Virginia	5.2
Wisconsin	2.9

(1) Data are not preliminary   (p) = preliminary.

A telltale sign of the strategic nature of the places where Donald Trump is making the most impact when it comes to job creation, especially in the manufacturing sector is the fact that only two states that did not vote for him in the 2016 presidential election—California and Illinois—featured in the list of the 10 states that contributed the most to the manufacturing job growth nationwide since 2017.

B: States with statistically significant unemployment rate changes from February 2018 to February 2019, seasonally adjusted as presented by the Department of Labor's Bureau of Labor Statistics:

State	Rate February 2018	Rate February 2019 (p)	Change (p)	Over-the-year
California	4.3	4.2	-0.1	
Colorado	2.9	3.7	.8	
Connecticut	4.5	3.8	-.7	
Delaware	4.0	3.4	-.6	
Hawaii	2.3	2.7	.4	
New York	4.5	3.9	-.6	
Oklahoma	3.8	3.3	-.5	
South Carolina	3.8	3.2	-.6	
Vermont	2.7	2.4	-.3	

(p) = preliminary.

C. States with statistically significant employment changes from February 2018 to February 2019, seasonally adjusted as presented by the Department of Labor's Bureau of Labor Statistics:

State	Rate February 2018	Rate February 2019 (p)	Change (p)	Over-the-year
Alabama	2,032,900	2,065,200	32,300	1.6
Arizona	2,828,500	2,905,400	76,900	2.7
California	17,100,200	17,322,700	222,500	1.3
Colorado	2,704,800	2,749,600	44,800	1.7
Florida	8,709,700	8,921,600	211,900	2.4
Georgia	4,507,700	4,604,800	97,100	2.2
Idaho	732,000	750,600	18,600	2.5
Illinois	6,103,300	6,162,400	59,100	1.0
Indiana	3,134,800	3,177,400	42,600	1.4
Kentucky	1,928,800	1,949,900	21,100	1.1
Michigan	4,406,300	4,447,500	41,200	.9
Nevada	1,370,400	1,418,800	48,400	3.5
New York	9,648,100	9,743,500	95,400	1.0
North Carolina	4,471,200	4,536,000	64,800	1.4
Oregon	1,903,700	1,933,200	29,500	1.5
South Carolina	2,140,800	2,171,900	31,100	1.5
South Dakota	437,600	446,200	8,600	2.0
Tennessee	3,043,500	3,096,500	53,000	1.7
Texas	12,393,600	12,662,400	268,800	2.2
Utah	1,502,900	1,546,600	43,700	2.9
Washington	3,379,100	3,445,800	66,700	2.0
West Virginia	719,300	736,800	17,500	2.4
Alabama				

(p) = preliminary.

Another impressive development over the past thirty months is the fall of the black unemployment rate. According to the Bureau of Labor Statistics, the overall civilian unemployment rate for African-Americans fell to 6.1 percent in June 2018, compared to 2.1 percent for Asian Americans, 3.4 percent for White Americans and 3.9 percent for Hispanics or Latinos. Judging further from the overall civilian unemployment rate in 2016 that was 4.9 percent—3.6 percent for Asian Americans, 4.3 percent for White Americans, 5.8 percent for Hispanics or Latinos, and 8.4 percent for Blacks or African Americans—it is easy to conclude that Donald Trump isn't one of those presidents that sticks his index finger in his mouth and then takes it out and holds it up in the air to get the direction of the wind (the mood of the people) before implementing his policies. Which leaves many wondering how much of a populist he is, as the mainstream media has been painting him to be.

When an October 2018 poll by Rasmussen Reports showed Donald Trump's approval rating among blacks hovering at 40%, many pundits who had not been favourable in their analysis of the 45th president of the United States of America questioned the authenticity of the poll, accusing the American polling company of always being favorable to Donald Trump in the past, and so could not be trusted. However, when other polls pointed out that the president could pick up about 20% of African American votes in the 2020 presidential election, compared to the 8% support he got from voters from this particular demographic group in 2016, they told a lot about the inroad the president has made within this community that has a strong history voting Democrats and the Democratic party.

III: Promise to Raise Tariffs on Imported Goods

The first two years of Donald Trump's presidency have shown that relations with Mexico and China, which are two of the United States of America's major trading partners, are not going to deteriorate to the point of no return that many people feared business affairs would degenerate into following the statement then-candidate Trump made to his supporters during a campaign rally in Tampa that "*Any country that devalues their currency in order to take unfair advantage of the United States, and all of its companies who can't compete, will face tariffs and taxes to stop the cheating. And when they see that, they will stop the cheating...*". It became obvious that things could be fixed shortly after Donald Trump's inauguration when the former US. Secretary of State Rex Tillerson and the secretary of Homeland Security John F. Kelly flew to Mexico on February 22, 2017, and held talks with the Mexican president Peña Nieto and other members of his administration. Mexican Foreign Secretary Luis Videgaray meeting with Donald Trump at the White House hardly three weeks after, marked a sobering period in US-Mexican relations under the Trump administration.

A tone down of the rhetoric against China after months of China-bashing that had reached fever-pitch during the election campaigns occurred following the meeting between the Chinese head of state Xi Jinping and Donald Trump in April 2017.

Those who after those meetings thought that the United States of America was not going to impose tariffs on goods made in China and Mexico, meant as countermeasures against those countries for their violation of trade agreements or for their engagement in unfair trade practices against the specifications of Section 301 of the Trade Act of 1974, were too optimistic. Bright-eyed pundits expected those meetings to act as a prelude to further meetings during which the USA, China, and Mexico were expected to renegotiate their business relationships. After all, Donald Trump considers it a disaster that more than 70,000 factories were lost in the USA due to their relocation to China since the Asian giant joined the World Trade Organization on December 11, 2001; he knows that cajoling those American companies to think of "America first" instead of punishing them, as well as Mexico and China, is the right way to go about mitigating the effects of the transfer of American manufacturing abroad, especially to these two low-cost countries.

By the start of 2018, many of the fears of a trade war with China and Mexico had been dispelled. The people should have seen that coming. After all, the US. President had even backtracked on his initial accusation of China as a currency manipulator, by telling The Wall Street Journal in April 2017 that *"They're not currency manipulators."*

Irrespective of how Trump skeptics, detractors, and supporters look at it, there is logic in this particular promise or pledge to introduce legislation establishing tariffs to *"discourage companies from laying off their workers in order to relocate to other countries, and then ship their manufactured products back to the U.S. tax-free"*, as the new US. President put it during his campaign. True he said legislation would be worked out within the first 100 days of his presidency, and true he grappled with it right after his inauguration. However, most of those who are experienced or versatile in international trade, international relations, and international law know that the process of putting in place the framework that would stop the flow of manufacturing jobs abroad would be long and complicated.

So, when the Trump presidency imposed tariffs on Canadian softwood lumber imports in late April 2017, a country that is the United States of America's closest neighbor and ally, those versed with that aspect of trade saw the potential for an escalation, especially against other countries. That is why when on March 8, 2018, Donald Trump proclaimed a 25 percent tariff on imported steel and a 10 percent tariff on imported aluminum, by citing section 232 of the Trade Expansion Act of 1962 that gives the executive branch the authority to investigate the effects that certain imports have on the country's national security and then adjust those imports as necessary, it became evident the president was upping the ante in the trade conflict. This was in line with a report by Commerce Secretary Wilbur Ross showing that during the past two decades, the domestic steel industry lost 35 percent of its jobs, while from 2013 and 2016, the aluminum industry experienced close to a 60 percent decrease in employment. However, when the president made exemptions for Canada and Mexico, some analysts thought he was prodding the USA's northern and southern neighbors on NAFTA. When two months later he rescinded the exemption on these two countries along with the European Union, his game plan became obvious to many. Today, we have the United States-Mexico-Canada Agreement (USMCA) in the picture. We can deduce from the above that China was the target of it all back in March 2018.

The world had to have seen it coming when on July 6, 2018, Donald Trump imposed tariffs on $34 billion in Chinese exports to the USA, prompting China to retaliate by placing similar tariffs on $34 billion worth of American goods. The additional 10 percent tariffs on $200 billion worth of Chinese imports that the US. President authorized a few days later on July 10, 2018, showed that Donald Trump has more up his sleeves in the trade war with China.

And that was the case. In January 2019, the United States announced 23 criminal charges against China's multinational technology company Huawei and its CFO Wanzhou Meng, outraging the Chinese government in the process. However, when the Trump administration upped the ante by raising the 10 percent tariffs on $200 billion worth of Chinese imports to 25% on grounds that China reneged on already agreed upon deals, it signaled an escalation that few people had seen coming. That is why his executive order ten days later restricting the export of U.S. information and communications technology to what the administration termed "foreign adversaries" was seen as targeting China. The Asian giant's response shortly after by raising tariffs on $60 billion worth of US goods did not surprise anyone. For now, there is a respite in the trade war between the United States of America and China after their leaders met at the G20 summit in Osaka last June 29, 2019, and agreed on a truce after extensive talks. Still, disagreements over the rules on foreign direct investment in China persist. The USA, like Japan and the countries of the European Union, thinks that the law on joint venture is responsible for the "leakage of intellectual property" to China, costing Western companies dearly. They also contend that it violates WTO rules that demand fair treatment of domestic and foreign companies.

IV: A Renegotiation of the Iran Nuclear Deal

It is doubtful at this stage that the 45th US. President would be able to fulfill his promises made during his campaign trail to renegotiate the Iran Nuclear Deal so that the United States of America would have greater control over the mechanisms that were put in place to make Iran comply with the agreement not to develop nuclear weapons and never to use nuclear energy for military purposes. Iran, so far, does not appear to be intimidated or lured by the promises or threats or even overtures made by the US. President to the North Korean dictator Kim Jong-un or by American military forays abroad, especially in Syria. So there are those who see Iran's unwillingness to renegotiate the Nuclear Deal it signed with the USA and other Western nations during the Obama presidency as an indication of the Middle Eastern nation's resolve not to be seen as a pushover.

Donald Trump's May 8, 2018 decision to pull the United States of America out of the Iran nuclear deal, which is a vindication of his pre-election statement that *"It is clear to me that we cannot prevent an Iranian nuclear bomb under the decaying and rotten structure of the current agreement,"* is seen by many not only as an audacious move but also as a calculation bordering on chutzpah. In fact, the USA's withdrawal from the treaty displeased America's closest allies and put the future of Iran's nuclear ambitions in doubt. True the deal failed to constrain Iran when it comes to the country's long-range missile program; true it failed to hold Iran responsible for not contributing to "…regional and international peace and security…" as exposed in its involvements in the civil wars in Syria and Yemen; and true the so-called "Sunset Provisions" in the deal appeared shortsighted since it made it possible for certain restrictions on Iran's nuclear weapon program to expire when those restrictions should have been made indefinite; however, the absence of a deal leaves the Middle East more unstable and more dangerous today than it was a year ago.

Some analyst are of the opinion that Americans manifest a cryptic nature towards the Iran issue because even though the majority of non-Americans deplore the United States of America's unilateral cancellation of the Iran deal by pulling out of it, most Americans believed the 45th president of the United States of America when he said that: *"This was a horribly one-sided deal that should have never, ever been made…It didn't bring calm, it didn't bring peace, and it never will."* Even so, most Americans are skeptical that Iran would be brought down to its knees even after the president tried to make them think so when in his harangue, he made known his position thus: *"…in a few moments, I will sign a presidential memorandum to begin reinstating U.S. nuclear sanctions on the Iranian regime. We will be instituting the highest level of economic sanction. Any nation that helps Iran in its quest for nuclear weapons can be sanctioned by the United States. "*

How things develop over the Iran riddle will become clearer in 2019, 2020 and beyond as relations with Russia and China become less hazy, and after the Trump administration's relations with the House of Representatives, the Senate, and the Supreme Court enter a new phase.

Unlike the unequivocal statement that Donald Trump made regarding the Iran deal when he said in his campaign promise that *"This deal if I win will be a totally different deal. This will be a totally different deal... ",* the reality on the ground seems to be indicating something different altogether. Many diplomatic and security experts agree that Iran is a hard nut to crack, and since no hasty steps are expected to be taken against it in an effort to make the ancient nation-state change its mind, the sanctions against Iran are thus expected to be there for years to come.

V: Rollback Obama's Cuba Deal

Rolling back the Cuban Deal that the Obama administration struck with Cuba's neo-communist government under the leadership of Raul Castro, the second Castro brother who is presiding over a country that has been America's No 1 enemy in the Western Hemisphere for close to six decades, would be another Herculean task for the president to accomplish if he sticks to his words to fulfill this particular campaign promise. As a matter of fact, Donald Trump was very succinct about Cuba, one reason why the Cuban Diaspora in America voted massively for him. When he said that *"The president's one-sided deal for Cuba and with Cuba benefits granted the Castro Regime was done through executive order, which means they can be undone and that is what I intend to do unless the Castro Regime meets our demands."*, he knew most Cuban-Americans were behind him in opposing the 44th US. President Barack Obama's Cuban deal.

Living with thawing relations with Cuba is a difficult pill to swallow for some Republicans, especially the party's elites who have made it part of their culture to hate if not despise the far-leftist system in place in Cuba and the Cuban elites who often hark back to the legacy of the Fidel Castro-led Cuban revolution, whose early years of survival was fraught with difficulties that they blame squarely on the Democratic administration of the 35th US. President John Fitzgerald "Jack" Kennedy. These Republican leaders never stopped holding onto the claim that the Kennedy administration failed to nip the communist regime of Fidel Castro in the bud. As a matter of fact, Fidel Castro and his band of revolutionaries made it to power on January 01, 1959 by ousting the regime of the US-backed dictator Fulgencio Batista, while Dwight Eisenhower, a Republican, was presiding over Affairs in the White House as the 34th president of the USA.

Another compelling argument against Republicans rests on the fact that the Eisenhower administration even recognized the new Cuban government. So, relations between the new Cuban authorities and Washington did not go awry until the Castro regime clamped down on Batista loyalists, and nationalized US. businesses, especially American oil refineries. These and other actions led the United States to impose an embargo on Cuba, starting with an arms embargo, and then to the commercial, economic and financial embargoes, before finally breaking off diplomatic relations with the new Havana authorities on January 3, 1961. Actually, when John F. Kennedy took over on January 20, 1961, he did not stop the previous administration's plan to use CIA-trained Cuban exiles for the invasion of Cuba. The Bay of Pigs invasion, as it became known, was unsuccessful, prompting Fidel Castro to use his strengthened position to declare Cuba a communist state, thereby forcing the hand of the Kennedy administration to overthrow the new communist regime through the secret "Operation Mongoose" program, and to even attempt an assassination of the Cuban strongman, all of which ended in failure.

Cuban-American relations have experienced ups and downs since 1961, beginning with:

- the 1962 Cuban Missile Crisis
- attempts by Democratic President Jimmy Carter to repair relations in 1977
- the 1980 flooding of US shores with roughly 125,000 Cubans—a good number of them convicts—when the Cuban government allowed all

those who wanted to leave the country to immigrate
- the 1991 collapse of Cuba's patron the Soviet Union
- the 1996 tightening of US. sanctions against the island following the shooting down of two US rescue planes over Cuban waters that resulted in the deaths of four people
- the Elian Gonzalez (a 6-year-old boy Cuban boy who survived a boat capsize that killed his mother who was trying to flee with him to Florida) international custody battle between Elian Gonzalez's father and the boy's relatives in Miami that ended with the boy returning to Cuba with his Cuban father
- the 2001 US. export of food to Cuba following 40 years of embargo, in response to the devastations of Hurricane Michelle
- the 2002 Bush administration's declaration of Cuba as a part of the "axis of evil" (meaning governments that the Republican administration accused of sponsoring terrorism and seeking weapons of mass destruction, a list that included Iran, Iraq, and North Korea, Cuba, Libya, and Syria) following charges that the Castro-regime was developing biological weapons
- the 2003 tightening of sanctions against Cuba to trigger the collapse of the Castro regime
- the 2008 change in leadership in Cuba and the USA with the stepping down of Fidel Castro, the rise of Raul Castro as the official president of Cuba, and the election of Barack Obama as the 44th US.

President of the United States of America

- the 2009 lifting of restrictions on family travel and remittances to Cuba, and the arrest of USAID contractor Alan Gross by the Cuban authorities on charges of espionage or for spying for the US. Government

- the 2011 release from US. Custody of Cuban agent Rene Gonzalez, a member of the group called Cuban Five—also known as the Miami Five (five Cuban intelligence officers)—whose members were convicted in Miami in September 1998 for conspiring to commit espionage and to commit murder, for acting as an agent of a foreign government, and for other activities deemed illegal in the United States. That was after the new Cuban government refused to release Alan Gross

- the famous 2013 handshake in Johannesburg, South Africa between US. President Barack Obama and Cuba's Raul Castro during the memorial service of Nelson Mandela, the renowned world's statesman, the South African icon and anti-Apartheid leader hero

- the 2014 reestablishment of diplomatic relations between the United States of America and Cuba, and the release of Alan Gross and his return to the USA

- and the 2015 removal of Cuba from the United States of America's list of countries sponsoring terrorism.

The fact that 58% of Americans in a March 2016 poll stated that they favor the diplomatic thaw initiated in December 2014, with 62% convinced that the re-opening of Cuban-American relations would be mostly good for the U.S, and with more than 60% voicing an interest to visit the Caribbean country, it is hard to imagine how Donald Trump would be able to satisfy his Republican base, especially the vocal Cuban exile community in Florida that opposes the thaw initiated by the previous administration.

If Donald Trump cannot fully satisfy this hard-line base, he certainly would not leave them empty-handed. That realization was more keenly observed in the June 16, 2017 rally in Miami's Little Havana neighborhood, where he dwelled lengthily on this topic, telling his supporters among other things the following *"…I am canceling the last administration's completely one-sided deal with Cuba…"*. However, it became obvious that he did not intend to reverse his predecessor's entire policy, and that he was, in fact, trying to hold the political elites in Cuba accountable for human-rights violations while pushing them to open up the Cuban economy. These objectives are highlighted in a White House Fact Sheet on the president's Cuban policy, which aims to:

- Enhance compliance with U.S. law, particularly provisions governing the Cuban embargo and ban on tourism
- Hold the Cuban regime accountable for oppression and human rights abuses
- Further the national security and foreign policy interests of the United States and Cuban people

- Empower Cubans to develop economic and political liberty.

It would take some time to realize the objectives above because the US. Treasury and Commerce Departments have to come up with new regulations that would align with the goals of the Trump administration. Irrespective of the Trump administration's bluster on Cuba, one thing for sure is that it does not intend to restore the "wet foot, dry foot" immigration policy that Barack Obama terminated during his last days in office. This particular policy allowed Cubans who landed on or touched U.S. soil to stay in the country and pursue residency a year after their arrival.

VI: Reformation of Social Security, Medicare, and Medicaid

The 45th US. President's promise not to make changes to Social Security, Medicaid, and Medicare, which is what most American voters want anyway, despite the fact that many in the Republican Party leadership want otherwise, has so far been kept, even though attempts have recently been made to enact some changes. Back in early 2017, Mick Mulvaney, the director of the Office of Management and Budget, said Donald Trump refused to make any changes to Social Security and Medicare while preparing his first budget request. The House Freedom Caucus chairman Mark Meadows (R-N.C.) who campaigned for

Donald Trump in the 2016 presidential election indicated that the president is resolute in his position, which is another way of saying that the president had effectively taken any Social Security or Medicare reforms off the table and that until conservatives "*make a more compelling case, he's not going there.*"

There are looming changes to Social Security all right as evidenced by the 2019 budget proposal that saw Donald Trump reviving a proposal to cut disability programs administered by social security under the fanciful blueprint called "Reform Disability Programs", which would see an $82 billion dollar reduction in spending over the next 10 years. This cutback would be coming from:

- Social Security Disability Insurance (or SSDI, which is an earned benefit that focuses on those with mental and physical impairments that are considered severe enough to prevent them from working for a minimum of 12 months or until their deaths)
- Supplemental Security Income (SSI), which is a program funded by general revenues collected by the Treasury Department that serves only those who have very limited income and assets by paying benefits to low-income people who are 65 years old or older, to certain adults who are disabled or blind, and to children who are disabled and blind.

However, while Social Security taxes paid by workers, employers and self-employed people funds SSDI and stands out in that its benefits can be paid to blind or disabled workers, it is similar to Social Security retirement benefits in that its benefits can also be paid to the close family members of the blind and disabled such as their children, their widows or widowers; and it can also be paid to those adults with disabilities since childhood who have not worked.

Another curious thing is that even though 2018 ended with the president keeping most of his promises on Medicare, especially with the government's responsibility for the program's funding staying in place without cuts to the services, major compromises have been made by the Trump administration. Compromises too have been made on Medicare over the next 10 years, especially when we take into account Donald Trump's 2019 budget proposal where spending would be cut cumulatively by $236 billion, with much of the focus being on "waste" and "fraud", and on making changes to the way the program prices drugs and pays for them.

Even though intentions have been voiced and attempts have been made to change certain aspects of Medicaid, the program remains unchanged. If the Trump administration wants to make changes to the program, Donald Trump would have to sign the White House's proposal to have the government spend an estimated $4.7 trillion on Medicaid over the next 10 years, compared with $5.3 trillion under current funding levels. Doing so would break his promise not to carry out any changes to Medicaid as well.

VII: Tax Cuts

As a nominee of the Republican Party during the 2016 presidential election campaign, Donald Trump pledged that within the first 100 days of his presidency, he would introduce tax reform legislation, reduce rates for the middle class and businesses, and simplify the tax code. So, when the United States Treasury Secretary Steven Mnuchin said on April 26, 2017, that Donald Trump's anticipated tax reforms would be *"the biggest tax cut and largest tax reform in history of this country,"* and when the then-House Speaker Paul Ryan also commented that *"progress is being made and we're moving and getting on the same page."*, their statements beguiled Americans and signaled a conflict between the tax reformers in the Trump administration and the Republicans on Capitol Hill who were insisting on contributing to the tax reform plan.

Many Congressional Republicans thought the president's April 2017 one-page handout on tax reform proposal lacked the crucial components they considered necessary in their push to accomplish the first major tax reform in more than 30 years. Republican Congressmen thought at the time that the top-line principles of the future plan failed to spell out the far-reaching reforms that they were looking forward to; that it skimped on important details like relations with the lobbyists, how to pay for it, how to get it through House and Senate, etcetera, etcetera. In a nutshell, the president wanted to cut individual tax rates—slashing the top rate from 39.6% to 35%—and reducing the number of total rates from seven to three. He also wanted to cut the top tax rate for all businesses to 15%, far below the top rates in the country before his presidential inauguration. That went in line with his promises during the campaign that he would lower individual income tax rates from today's rates of 10%, 15%, 25%, 28%, 33%, 35%, and 39.6%, to three tax brackets of 10%, 20%, and 25%. However, he changed his mind later and promised to match what House Republicans had been calling for—that is, rates at 12%, 25%, and 33% respectively.

When it came to lowering business rates, he initially wanted to bring it down to 15%, well below today's top rate of 35% for corporations, and 39.6% for owners and shareholders of so-called pass-through businesses (where the owners and shareholders report profits on their personal tax returns) such as small shops, law firms and hedge funds. However, what we have now is the Corporate Income Tax Rate of 21 percent, which is similar to those levied by most of the major economies of the world.

Other aspects of the tax reforms the president had in mind included One-Time Tax on overseas profits (the creation of a 10-percent repatriation tax), a switch to a Territorial Tax system, no Border Adjustment Tax that the House Republicans proposed, Tax break for childcare costs, the elimination of all deductions except those for mortgage interest and charitable contributions; and the repeal of the Alternative Minimum Tax, the Estate Tax and the 3.8% Medicare Tax. Since it became obvious that many things in those proposals did not add up, people were not surprised by the reaction from the Republicans on Capitol Hill who among other things questioned the president's tax reform proposal for failing to include the border adjustment tax that many of them favored.

Many on both sides of the political divide agree that the president compromised on the matter of tax reform. That is why when the Senate and the House passed the final version of the tax bill on December 19 and 20, 2017, making it possible for the president to sign it into law two days after, it marked the most consequential tax legislation in three decades.

What comes out of the reform is the fact that on average, every income group would pay less in taxes from 2019-2027, even though not everyone would benefit from it.

As independent tax analysts and the Joint Committee on Taxation have pointed out, 2027 would be a turning point because every income group below $75,000 will see an actual increase in taxation, leaving only those with income ranges above $75,000 as the real beneficiaries of Donald Trump's tax reform. From its analysis whose depth cannot be questioned, the Tax Policy Center provides a gloomier analysis that leaves a sour note in the mouths of the middle and lower classes by revealing that taxpayers higher than the 90th percentile of the population—meaning those who earn about $225,000 and above—are the ones, without doubt, to get a tax cut in 2027.

In a nutshell, the new tax legislation provides tax relief for all income groups, and for most taxpayers within each of the groups. However, it fails to provide tax relief to "everybody," and leaves most taxpayers (all in the lower class and most in the middle class) paying more in taxes in

2027 than would have been the case if the law had not changed.

List of countries by tax revenue to GDP ratio

Country	Tax as % of GDP
Afghanistan	6.4
Albania	22.9
Algeria	7.7
Angola	5.7
Argentina	37.2
Armenia	22.0
Australia	25.8
Austria	43.4
Azerbaijan	17.8
Bahamas, The	18.7
Bahrain	4.8
Bangladesh	8.5
Barbados	32.6
Belarus	24.2
Belgium	47.9
Belize	21.6
Benin	15.4
Bhutan	10.7
Bolivia	27.0
Bosnia and Herzegovina	41.2
Botswana	35.2
Brazil	34.4
Bulgaria	27.8
Burkina Faso	11.5
Burma	4.9
Burundi	17.4
Cambodia	8.0
Cameroon	18.2
Canada	32.2
Cape Verde	23.0

Chad	4.2
Chile	21.0
China[4] [5]	28.1
Colombia	16.1
Comoros	12.0
Congo, Republic of	5.9
Costa Rica	21.0
Côte d'Ivoire	15.3
Croatia	36.7
Cuba	44.8
Cyprus	39.2
Czech Republic	36.3
Denmark	50.8
Djibouti	20.0
Dominica	30.3
Dominican Republic	12.0
Congo, Democratic Republic of	13.2
Ecuador	13.2
Egypt	15.8
El Salvador	13.3
Equatorial Guinea	1.7
Estonia	32.3
Ethiopia	11.6
European Union[7]	35.7
Fiji	21.8
Finland	43.6
France	47.9
Gabon	10.3
Gambia, The	18.9
Georgia	21.7
Germany	40.6
Ghana	20.8
Greece	39.0
Guatemala	11.9
Guinea	8.2
Guinea-Bissau	11.5
Guyana	31.9
Haiti	9.4

Honduras	15.6
Hong Kong	13.0
Hungary	39.1
Iceland	40.4
India	17.7
Indonesia	12.0
Iran	6.1
Ireland	30.8
Israel	36.8
Italy	43.5
Jamaica	27.2
Japan	28.3
Jordan	21.1
Kazakhstan	26.8
Kenya	18.4
Kiribati	20.7
Korea, South	26.8
Kuwait	1.5
Kyrgyzstan	21.4
Laos	10.8
Latvia	30.4
Lebanon	14.4
Lesotho	42.9
Liberia	13.2
Libya	2.7
Lithuania	20.9
Luxembourg	36.5
Macau, China	20.1
Macedonia	29.3
Madagascar	10.7
Malawi	20.7
Malaysia	15.5
Maldives	20.5
Mali	15.3
Malta	35.2
Mauritania	15.4
Mauritius	19.0
Mexico	19.7

Federated States of Micronesia	12.3
Moldova	33.8
Mongolia	33.8
Montenegro	28.0
Morocco	22.3
Mozambique	13.4
Namibia	28.8
Nepal	10.9
Netherlands	39.8
New Zealand	34.5
Nicaragua	17.8
Niger	11.0
Nigeria	6.1
Norway	43.6
OECD[9]	34.8
Oman	2.0
Pakistan	16.8
Panama	10.6
Papua New Guinea	24.5
Paraguay	12.0
Peru	18.0
Philippines	14.4
Poland	33.8
Portugal	37.0
Qatar	2.2
Taiwan	13.0
Romania	27.7
Russia	19.5
Rwanda	14.1
Saint Lucia	23.1
Saint Vincent and the Grenadines	26.5
Samoa	25.5
São Tomé and Príncipe	17.4
Saudi Arabia	5.3
Senegal	19.2
Serbia	34.1
Seychelles	32.0

Sierra Leone	10.5
Singapore	14.2
Slovakia	29.5
Slovenia	39.3
Solomon Islands	24.7
South Africa	26.9
Spain	37.3
Sri Lanka	11.6
Sudan	6.3
Suriname	22.1
Swaziland	39.8
Sweden	45.8
Switzerland	29.4
Syria	10.7
Tajikistan	16.5
Tanzania	12.0
Thailand	17.0
Togo	15.5
Tonga	27.0
Trinidad and Tobago	28.0
Tunisia	14.9
Turkey	24.9
Turkmenistan	20.2
Uganda	12.6
Ukraine	28.1
United Arab Emirates	1.4
United Kingdom	34.4
United States	26.0
Uruguay	23.1
Uzbekistan	21.0
Vanuatu	17.8
Venezuela	25.0
Vietnam	13.8
Yemen	7.1
Zambia	16.1
Zimbabwe	27.2

VIII: Establish a ban on Muslims entering the U.S

The most controversial of all of Donald Trump's campaign promises is what many call "The Ban on Muslims Entering the United States of America." Even though the 45th US. president claims it is an effort to combat radical Islamic terrorism, his opponents do not think so, seeing it as a reflection of something deeper. Some even go further by accusing the president of harboring anti-Muslim biases. Actually, his first public statement in this regard, which was made during the primaries, said the following: *"Donald J. Trump is calling for a complete and total shutdown of Muslims entering the United States until our country's representatives can figure out what the hell is going on...We have no choice. We have no choice."*

When he switched to "extreme vetting" after he became the Republican Party's presidential candidate, it was an indication of the impracticality of his former position. After all, many Muslim countries like Saudi Arabia, Qatar, United Arab Emirates, Kuwait, and Jordan are staunch allies of the United States of America.

The fact that Donald Trump kept changing his stance on this issue by expanding on his "Exemption List" confirms the sensitivity of the topic. Many people still describe it as a Muslim ban, even though he did not explicitly state it that way. In fact, what he actually said was that he would *"suspend immigration from terror-prone regions where vetting cannot safely occur. All vetting of people coming into our country will be considered 'extreme vetting.'"*

This pledge was clearly spelled out on January 27, 2017, when he signed an executive order that temporarily placed a ban on immigration from Iran, Iraq, Libya, Somalia, Syria, Sudan, and Yemen. Particularly jarring was fact that the ban on Syrian refugees too was indefinite even though the United States of America under Donald Trump's predecessor Barack Obama had pledged to take in some of the Syrian refugees languishing in camps in the Middle East, North Africa, and Europe.

It is foolhardy to imagine, let alone believe that the president's campaign promise to place a temporary ban on Muslims entering the United States of America has not been resisted by the Judiciary branch of the US. government strongly enough. In his January 27, 2017, Executive Order on *"Protecting the Nation from Foreign Terrorist Entry into the United States"*, by banning citizens of seven majority-Muslim countries from entering the United States of America, the Trump administration got a decisive rebuff from a federal appellate court that halted the enforcement of the decree. Even the second executive order he signed on March 6, 2017, which exempted permanent legal residents and applied only to future visa applicants, and not to those who already hold valid visas, was rebuffed ten days later on March 26, 2017, the very day that it was supposed to go into effect, by two federal judges who ruled against the revised travel ban, even though Iraq was taken off the list. That pushback showed once again that they did not believe the Trump administration's claim that the immigration ban was not based on religion, but rather on national security concerns.

The federal judges were not the only legal bodies that opposed Donald Trump in this regard. The Hawaiian U.S. District Judge Derrick Watson issued a nationwide temporary restraining order. His position was that the new executive order and its predecessor contained *"significant and unrebutted evidence of religious animus driving the promulgation"*, that it *"began life as a Muslim ban,"* and that statements made by Trump and his advisers *"provide direct evidence of the Executive Order's discriminatory motivations."*

The fact that the White House did not appeal to the Supreme Court against the travel ban halt, and the fact that the second or revised ban in March 2017 was blocked from implementation by U.S. District Judge Derrick Watson, as well as by a federal judge in Hawaii, indicated that Donald Trump's promise to temporarily "ban Muslims" from entering the USA would be difficult to fulfill.

As a matter of fact, even though the Trump executive orders were not welcomed by many people in different quarters of the bureaucracy, the actions by the courts blocking them prompted counter-protests across the country by people who thought the courts had become a part of the unresponsive establishment doing little or nothing to protect the United States of America from global terrorism led by Islamic jihadi groups such as Al-Qaeda, ISIS, Boko Haram, etcetera.

So, when in June 2018, based on a 5-4 decision, the U.S. Supreme Court upheld the third version of the travel ban, which is a watered-down version of Trump's Muslim ban promise, it spelled a heavy blow to Donald Trump's campaign promise, though the Trump administration apparently came out of it unscathed. This particular version restricts the entry into the USA of nationals of North Korea, Iran, Libya, Somalia, Syria, Venezuela, and Yemen. Five of these countries are Muslim-majority except North Korea and Venezuela. Of note is the fact that the US. Congress and/or other previous US. administrations had designated these countries individually or in group(s) as states posing national security risks to the United States of America. Curiously enough, the combined Muslim population of those countries in the ban list constitutes only 8 percent of the world's Muslim population.

The U.S. Supreme Court Chief Justice John Roberts would sound a conciliatory note when he echoed the court's majority opinion that Donald Trump's directive was *"...facially neutral toward religion..."* What is even more telling about the whole issue was his own opinion when he wrote among other things that *"The proclamation is expressly premised on legitimate purposes: preventing entry of nationals who cannot be adequately vetted and inducing other nations to improve their practices...The text says nothing about religion."*

People exempted from the new rules are those with business or educational ties to the United States of America; as well as those entering the country with a parent, a spouse, a fiancé, a child, a son-or daughter-in-law, or a sibling, including step-siblings or half-siblings residing in the USA. Though this compromise did not meet the expectations of many Trump supporters who were rooting for a complete ban, it is considered as a big win by those who knew from the onset that a complete ban was impossible.

The conclusion is that even though Donald Trump failed to realize his promise of a "total and complete shutdown" of Muslims entering the United States, he managed to use his executive orders to restrict the entry to the USA of people from Muslim countries that even previous administrations considered high-risk states.

IX: Rapprochement with Russia

The most controversial of all the promises Donald Trump made while campaigning in the run-up to the 2016 presidential election and the one that has been the most difficult to keep or fulfill is a rapprochement with Russia and a review of America's burdensome military ties with its foreign allies, especially the members of the military alliance called the North Atlantic Treaty Organization (NATO).

Desirable though it is, Donald Trump had to have known that his quest to resume harmonious and working relations with the Eurasian giant to "what it was" in the 1990s, following the collapse in December 1991 of the USSR (Union of Soviet Socialist Republics) of which Russia was the dominant constituent republic, was not going to go down well with the dogs of war within the military/industrial complex and within the political establishment that viewed the resurging Russia under Vladimir Putin as a threat to America's position as the world's sole superpower after 1991. Variously described as Russophobes, Cold-War hawks, globalists and "people of the Deep State", these opponents of Vladimir Putin's Russia are bent on seeing to it that Russia never resurges again, and that Russia's President Vladimir Putin who is overseeing its resurgence, lose control of the country to Russian liberals whose ilks determined affairs in the Kremlin during the 1990s when Russia kowtowed to the USA and its Western Allies. Putin supporters, Putin apologists and those who disapprove of the United States of America's unfettered hegemony and its role in the new Cold War hold that America's military/industrial complex and its political establishment never forgave Russia's Vladimir Putin for questioning America's hegemony during his February 10, 2007 speech at the Munich Security Conference where he accused the USA of its *"almost uncontained hyper use of force in international relations"* and of its monopolistic dominance in global relations. Putin promised then and in later speeches such as the Crimean Speech and the Valdai Speech that Russia would take measures to ensure its security and sovereignty.

Russia's subservience to the West in the 1990s and the first years of this century was after a scary period of four decades when the USSR as the other superpower that emerged from the Second World War following the defeat of Nazi Germany and its allies, challenged US hegemony in the world, a rivalry that resulted in what is called *The Cold*

War, which is defined as a state of political hostility between the Soviet Union/its allies and the USA/its Western allies—a Cold War that was characterized by threats, propaganda, and other measures short of open warfare.

As a matter of fact, those who, just like Donald Trump, are alarmed by the recent descent into a "New Cold War" following years of deteriorating US-NATO relations with Russia, are not in the minority. However, they appear to be the silent or "silenced" majority. They range from former US. Secretary of State Henry Kissinger; Sovietologists like Stephen Frand Cohen—professor emeritus of Russian studies at Princeton University and New York University; Diplomats like Jack Foust Matlock Jr. who is the former US. Ambassador to the USSR from October 26, 1981-February 20, 1987, and renowned artists like Steven Seagal. We also find in this list scientists, scholars, journalists, intellectuals and common folks with an understanding of geopolitics and history. These are people who like Francis Fukuyama, an American political scientist, political economist, and author who considered the end of the last Cold-War in 1989, and the collapse of the USSR two years later as the beginning of a new era that would result in the establishment of a "universal and homogenous" state. Fukuyama summed up that expectation best when he wrote in his 1992 book entitled *"The End of History"* that:

> *What we may be witnessing is not just the end of the Cold War, or the passing of a particular period of*

post-war history, but the end of history as such: that is, the endpoint of mankind's ideological evolution and the universalization of Western liberal democracy as the final form of human government.

Right from day one after Donald Trump won the 2016 presidential elections the mainstream media, Trump detractors and opponents, and more especially the elites of both the Republican and Democratic Parties never stopped harping on the points that Russia had a hand in Donald Trump's 2016 victory, allegations centered around what is called "Collusion with Russia, but which the Trump administration calls "Fake News". Some of these points include claims that:

- Russia tampered with the 2016 presidential election through hacking
- Russian President Vladimir Putin and Russian agents conspired with WikiLeaks in the release of damaging information to the world about Hilary Clinton's campaign malpractices and the United States of America in general
- media outlets such as RT (Russia Today) and Vesti News that are considered by the United State of America's security apparatus to be nothing but Russia's propaganda tools, along with the social media and extensive trolling sponsored by Russia, have been spreading false information that are damaging to US. interests at home and abroad
- Russian interference in the election was all about making sure that Hillary Clinton lost and that

Trump became the president with the task of smoothening US-Russian relations.

The collusion line is all the more controversial because the Trump camp rejects it vehemently as a distraction. The claims of collusion are based on the allegation that Donald Trump and even his appointees and members of his retinue had illegal dealings with Russian officials prior to and just after the 2016 presidential vote. And since the accusations or allegations degenerated to the point where some of Donald Trump's opponents called or are still calling him a Putin puppet, it is not surprising that the pushback from the Trump administration has helped to polarize the country even further as both antagonizing camps are going about denigrating, belittling and exposing one another, giving the public a better understanding of their underhand actions and agendas.

The pushback the 45th and current President has been experiencing comes with such a high degree of virulence that a fair percentage of Americans now think Donald Trump would be impeached before the end of his four-year term in office. The Trump hysteria has been coming from the mainstream media, the members of the former administration of Barack Obama, as well as from those who are opposed to his idea of rapprochement with Russia, especially the warmongers, Cold War hawks, anti-'Putinists", Russophobes, neoconservatives who are popularly known as neocons, and some libertarians who saw and continue to see Russia as the United States of America's No 1 geostrategic enemy. Some pundits and most Trump supporters call this talk of Russia's "nefarious" plan against America "Hysteria", but be it "Anti-Russia Hysteria" or not, it has fettered whatever plans Donald Trump had in mind on improving relations with Russia, even though it is unlikely that it has completely killed the idea of a rapprochement with Russia. True it became difficult during the first weeks of the Trump presidency to imagine that the new American president would be able to honor his campaign promise to work with Russia in defeating religious terrorist groups like ISIS, in tackling the destabilizing effect of uncontrolled immigration and in dealing with other factors threatening world peace and harmony. However, the purported use of chemical weapons by Syrian President Bashar Al-Assad, and the April 07, 2017 American response by bombing the Syria Al-Shayrat airfield with 59 Tomahawk missiles fired from a US destroyer in the Mediterranean Sea following Donald Trump's orders, had the effect of tranquilizing most of the president's opponents. For a while after the Syrian attack, the mainstream media mellowed in its criticism of the US. president, the hostilities from established politicians even seemed to have abated or disappeared altogether, and most Americans were mortified if not awed. It suddenly dawned on the average person that by doing what those who opposed him wanted him to do, especially by appearing to be confrontational to Putin's Russia through the bombing of Russia's client state—Syria, Donald Trump fell in line with the game-plan of the so-called "Guardians of the State", the purported shadowy forces determining America's direction. Many Americans started thinking that he was beginning to do the bidding of the elites of the political establishment that are also drawn from the ranks of the Republican Party and the Democratic Party.

When in the aftermath of the Syrian strike Donald Trump and his secretary of state Rex Tillerson, and the Russian president Vladimir Putin and his foreign minister Sergey Lavrov all agreed in their separate statements that US-Russian relations were at their all-time worst, Americans, Russians and citizens of other countries of the world started having doubts about the 45th US. President's election campaign promise to have warm ties with Russia.

Yes, it is very difficult for Donald Trump to take new steps toward finding common ground with Russia. We only have to look back at the early months of the Trump presidency when in late July 2017, a strong bipartisan bill overwhelmingly sailed through the House of Representatives by 419-3 votes, giving Congress the power to block any action by the White House that would weaken sanctions on Russia. This was after the initial version passed through the Senate on a 98-2 vote. Many people found it intriguing that the four members of the Republican Party and the one Democratic Party member who voted against the bill were all lawmakers reputed for their transparency and for supporting issues based on humanity and not based on unqualified interests. Pundits were surprised that Donald Trump signed this bipartisan bill on August 03, 2017. They had every reason to because the new law heaped new sanctions on Russia, Iran, and North

Korea, even though the bill was a direct challenge to the president's authority.

So after fettering the president with a bill that some analyst consider a noose that he was compelled to put around his neck with his own hands by signing it into a law, it came as no surprise that the idea of a Trump-Putin summit after that new rule left room for varied speculations, even though hardly anyone would disagree on the need for the two countries to find common ground by working together in a world that is growing more unpredictable every day. These two powers need to look into:

- US-Russian relations centered around resolving their differences and setting new rules of diplomatic and military engagements that would lessen if not eliminate geopolitical tensions around the world
- the opportunities for both nations to exploit by working together for the welfare of their citizens
- the need to deal with the common threats out there in the rest of the world, common threats that stand to jeopardize not only their individual and collective interests, but also their security and the security of the world at large, especially in the fight against terrorism, drugs, international crime, human trafficking and illegal immigration.

Still, many pundits with few if any bipartisan biases and an outlook on geopolitics that dwell more on what is good for humanity than for "US. Interests" only, see this all-time low in US-Russian relations as a step backward that gives both the Trump and Putin administrations more room to maneuver and take a bigger leap forward in improving US-Russian relations, a development that would set the stage for a new era in world affairs where the United States of America would be the dominant power but not the only superpower, an era that could otherwise be called a multi-polar world.

So the fact that Trump detractors, especially his opponents of the Democratic Party and of some of the mainstream media he calls fake news, view all past Trump-Putin meetings with suspicion, to the point of even alleging that the US. president is taking Putin's side on the issue of how to go about improving US-Russian relations at a time that they think Russia is failing to prove it did nothing to undermine the democratic process in the USA in 2016 as it claims, underpins the depth of what some consider a full-blown "Anti-Russia Hysteria" that is haunting the political establishment or that is being promoted by it. The Trump camp holds that the desire by powerful anti-Trump forces to drown the president in an imaginary conspiracy with Russia is so deep-seated that despite Donald Trump's exoneration by the report of the 2017- 2019 Special Counsel investigation, which is popularly called the Mueller Investigation, his opponents in the mainstream media and the Democratic Party still do not want to accept the law enforcement and counterintelligence investigation's findings on whether the Russian government interfered in the 2016 presidential election and colluded with the Trump campaign team against his rival Hillary Clinton.

Some pro-Trump pundits even go further by attributing cognitive dissonance to the anti-Trump camp's refusal to believe that the Trump campaign team did not collude with Russia in undermining the electoral process, or in tampering with the results of the 2016 US. presidential election as confirmed by the Mueller report. This leaves many people wondering whether US-Russian relations can improve under a battered Trump administration that is shackled by Congress, even if the American president wants it to.

The American scholar Stephen Frand Cohen underscores the difficulties Donald Trump has in forging better relations with Russia in an era of a "New Cold War" where the mechanisms to manage this state of political hostility between US-NATO on the one hand and Russia on the other hand, are non-existent, something which was not the case in the previous cold-war that lasted for forty-plus years between US-NATO and the USSR and its client states. The absence of these mechanisms aggravates the situation, especially at a time that more destructive weapons are being developed by USA-NATO on the one hand and Russia, China, Iran, India, and Pakistan on the other hand. However, even Stephen Cohen too, whom the mainstream media has been calling a Russian apologist, stands exonerated by the Mueller report as indicated by this excerpt of an August 2018 interview by Max Boot, a CNN Global Affairs Analyst:

COHEN: I have no idea what Mr. Boot is talking about. He wants Trump to threaten Russia? Why would we threaten Russia? You've got two nuclear --

BOOT: Because they're attacking us, Professor Cohen. Russia is attacking us right now according to Trump's own director of National Intelligence.

COHEN: I've been studying Russia for 45 years. I've lived in Russia, and I've lived here.

COHEN: Excuse me. What did you say to me?

BOOT: I said you've been consistently apologizing to Russia in those last 45 years?

COHEN: Right, I don't do defamation of people. I do serious analysis of serious national security problems. When people like you call people like me, and not only me, but people more eminent than me, apologists for Russia because we don't agree with your analysis, you are criminalizing diplomacy and detente and you are the threat to American national security end of story. Why do you have to defame somebody you don't agree with? They used to do that in the old Soviet Union. We don't do that here, where we used to, but we need to stop it.

COOPER: So, finally -- just finally Stephen, you're saying Russia was not attacking the United States?

COHEN: I know what you're talking about. They didn't -- during the 2016 election, Russia attacked the United

States. Yes, I don't think they attacked the United States.

BOOT: OK. And yet you just denied being an apologist for Russia. You're apologizing for Russia as we speak.

COHEN: Well, you haven't let me finish. You don't know what I'm going to say.

COOPER: Please go ahead.

COHEN: The meddling began, Mr. Cooper, and -- the meddling began right after the Russian revolution when Woodrow Wilson sent American troops to fight in the Russian civil war.

BOOT: Oh, please.

COHEN: The meddling began on the Soviet and Russians -- let me finish. On the meddling side when the communists formed communists international 1919, ever since then, Moscow has meddled in our politics. We have meddled in theirs. This is low-level stuff that went on. It is not an attack. It is not 9/11. It is not Pearl Harbor. It is not Russian paratroopers descending on Russia. This kind of hyperbole and attack on America suggests we need to attack Russia. So you've got Mr. Boot saying that Trump should threaten Russia. With what? Does he want to attack?

BOOT: Try sanctions.

COHEN: I think that Mr. Boot would have been happy if Trump had water-boarded Putin at the summit and made him confess. Trump carried out an act of diplomacy fully consistent with the history of American presidencies. Let us see what comes of it. Then judge.

COOPER: All right, Stephen Cohen, Max Boot, appreciate it. Thank you very much.

COHEN: Thank you.

Despite all the constraints on the Trump administration by a Congress that is bent on isolating Russia or forcing it to capitulate, a strong view held by some pundits is that the United States of America needs Russia in an era of a rising China, a retreat(tactical or otherwise) of globalism and of the inevitability of multipolarism due to the resurgence of Russia, as well as the rise of other centers of power such as China, India, and Brazil.

X: Build a Safe Zone for Refugees from Syria

One of the imminent points in Donald Trump's list of campaign promises that he was very succinct about and that marked a new idea on Syria was his statement that:

> *"They should build a safe zone. Take a big piece of land in Syria and they have plenty of land, believe*

me. Build a safe zone for all these people, because I have a heart, I mean these people, it's horrible to watch. But, they shouldn't come over here. We should build a safe zone."

In a nutshell, when then future 45th president of the United States of America made that statement, he was making a point that he did not want Syrian refugees ferried to safety in the USA, but wanted safe zones provided for them in their country—Syria. This was contrary to the position held by the former administration of Barack Obama that had regime change in Syria as its number one priority and that was okay with the idea of the United States of America admitting some 110,000 refugees into the country, with more than 10% of them coming from Syria.

However, the April 2017 US. strike on Syria regime forces, Russia's strengthening of Syria's air defenses after that, and the decline in cooperation between Russia and the USA in Syria against ISIS were major indicators of the setback in the US. President's election promise on mitigating the effects of Syria's refugee problems, though not the defeat of ISIS. That is why the implementation of the Syrian Deal hammered out in Astana, Kazakhstan between Russia, Turkey, and Iran on May 06, 2017, establishing de-escalation zones effectively left the USA out, something that might not have been the case had there not been the April 2017 US attack on Syria.

Even so, the reality on the ground today shows that the hard-line Islamic militant group whose objective was to carve out an Islamic Caliphate in the Middle East, North

Africa and Central Asia, has not only been cleansed in Iraq, but has also been defeated in Syria by pro-Russia regime forces and the American-supported Kurdish militias, thereby effectively eliminating the nucleus of the planned Islamic Caliphate and killing the nascent project.

Today, Donald Trump's Syrian fiasco is compounded by the fact that even though he sees the fight against ISIS in Syria and Iraq over, the military/industrial complex and the political establishment thinks America still has unfinished business in Syria, and so oppose or object to the president's stated objective to withdraw American troops from the Levantine country.

XI: Build a Border Wall that Mexico will Pay for

Apparently, 'Building a wall' along the entire Mexican/US border is controversial. When the idea was first mentioned, it triggered raised eyebrows and gasps of bewilderment from many quarters. Those who oppose it claim the whole idea smacks of chauvinism, and that it is replete with elements of racism, especially since the Trump team never talked of plans to build a fence along the Canadian-American border as well. What the 45th president of the United States of America has in mind is a 1,000-mile wall on the U.S-Mexico border, which at the moment has about 650 miles of existing barriers dominated by fences, with most of the barriers built during the presidencies of George W. Bush and Barack Obama. No extensions took place during the first twenty-four months of the Trump presidency, even though some of the fences or walls have been upgraded during the last two years. It wasn't until the end of February 2019 that a contractor called SLSCO began building six miles of an all-new wall in Hidalgo County, Texas, near the McAllen-Reynosa border crossing based on a contract with U.S. Army Corps of Engineers to build a total of 35 miles of wall this year in Texas and California, for $432 million.

According to a 2017 internal report by the Department of Homeland Security, the cost of building the wall is expected to rise to about $21.5bn, which is much higher than the president's estimated price tag of $12bn. Complicated further in April 2017 was a lawsuit from an environmental group signaling what could be considered the opening of the Pandora Box. Since then, there have been protests by landowners against a "government land grab", spelling more trouble ahead for Donald Trump's pledge to build the wall. Compounded even further was the fact that the deadline for bids from American and foreign contractors passed without much ado, and as a result, the federal government failed in its plans to announce the names of the companies to be hired to build prototypes of the wall by June 01, 2017. Magal Security Systems, the Israeli company that built the West Bank barrier happened to be one of such companies and is viewed by many pundits as ideally placed to do it.

What makes the idea of a border wall even more intriguing was Donald Trump's promise that within the first 100 days of his presidency, he would introduce legislation that would, as he said, "fully" fund the *"construction of a wall on our southern border with the full understanding that the country of Mexico will be reimbursing the United States for the full cost of such wall."* Before that, it was *"I would build a great wall, and nobody builds walls better than me, believe me, and I'll build them very inexpensively. I will build a great great wall on our southern border and I'll have Mexico pay for that wall."*

Mexico is not going to pay for the wall, a position it has made known in unequivocal terms. And with the price tag to build this wall standing at about $22 Billion of American taxpayers' money, it is no wonder that there are voices questioning the worthiness of a wall on America's southern border. So, the question is:

What is to be done now that Donald Trump appears truly serious about his promise to erect a wall to stem the flow of immigrants across America's southern border with Mexico?

Donald Trump requested funding from Congress for the wall in his first budget proposal in March 2017, a fact confirmed by the director of Donald Trump's Office of Management and Budget Mick Mulvaney who said that month that the president wanted the bicameral legislature of the federal government of the United States to put $1.5 billion toward his border wall in a supplemental spending bill in 2017 and $2.6 billion in 2018, totaling $4.1 billion over two years. The 45th president of the United States of America never got that wish.

True a fairly high percentage of Americans and most in the Trump administration and in Congress don't see the construction of a barrier along the border with Mexico as a priority for now, but it is going ahead. This despite the fact that the most recent version of the spending bill from the US Congress included new border security funding, but did not state funding the building of a border wall. In fact, the December 22, 2018 to January 25, 2019 (35 days) partial shutdown of the federal government as a result of Donald Trump's decision not to sign any spending bill that did not include $5.7 billion to build the wall, and the unwillingness of Democrats in Congress to vote for a bill providing that money said a lot about the tug-of-war around the promise to build a wall along the Mexican-American border, which the 45th president of the United States made as a presidential candidate.

Since Donald Trump regards the idea of a border wall as a patriotic endeavor for the sake of America's security, it is not surprising that there are Trump supporters and critics out there who fault him for being open to buy foreign services to what they too consider a patriotic endeavor in building the wall, especially when he once said that *"We are going to do everything in our power to make sure that more products are stamped with those wonderful words 'Made in the USA'. That's why I am here today. In just a few moments, I will be signing a "Buy American and Hire American' executive order. You haven't heard about that in a long time in this country. With this action, we are sending a powerful signal to the world."*

To prevent foreign firms from bidding, all the Donald Trump administration had to do was suspend the Government Procurement Agreement (GPA) with the WTO. A US president can withdraw from the GPA by giving 60 days' notice with no liability. But that would have gone against the World Trade Organization which is an offspring of the Bretton Woods Conference.

XII: Repeal "Obamacare"

Donald Trump's campaign promise to repeal and replace "Obamacare", the Patient Protection and Affordable Care Act that is often shortened to Affordable Care Act (ACA) and nicknamed "Obamacare", was expected to haunt him from the get-go since it involved doing away with a health care reform law that has been the most comprehensive in the history of the United States of America, and that has had the greatest impact in uplifting the health of Americans over a short period of time than any other before it. As a matter of fact, it is a major positive outcome from the long-overdue reformation of the US. health system. With analysts pointing out right from the very beginning that fulfilling that particular campaign promise would take the country away from the Affordable Care Act's goal to get more people covered at a price they can afford, the Trump team and Republicans, in general, should have known that they were giving themselves a Herculean task to fulfill.

Since no one can dispute the fact that individuals and

people, in general, are never happy when they are deprived of their benefits or when others take actions that roll back the progress made in their lives or wellbeing, it doesn't take a rocket scientist to figure it out that the average man in the street expects a better replacement for the Affordable Care Act (ACA), if the Trump administration and the Republicans are serious about replacing it. In short, Man does not expect to move backward in life. People move up, not down. "Obamacare" was an improvement on Health Insurance in the USA, which still lags behind most developed countries of the world when it comes to the effectiveness of medical cost-sharing that health plans are supposed to guarantee. That is why Americans expect their health plans to improve even further from the level that "Obamacare" has upgraded them to; that is why most Americans expect the repeal of "Obamacare" to bring about a far better plan, something that the opponents of the Affordable Care Act (ACA) have so far failed to come up with.

Yes, in his campaign promise, Donald Trump pledged to introduce legislation to "repeal and replace" the Affordable Care Act, within the first 100 days of his presidency. But that did not stop many Americans from wondering whether the GOP was oblivious of the raised standards brought about by ACA when in early March 2017, the Republican leaders in the House introduced a bill, publicly backed by Donald Trump and the White House, called the American Health Care Act that was supposed to repeal and replace "Obamacare", and then set about negotiating with members of Congress to win their support to pass it. However, on

March 24, 2017, the Republican leaders pulled the bill from the floor after realizing that they lacked the votes to pass it because no Democrat would vote for it and some members of the conservative House Freedom Caucus and Republican moderates in the Tuesday Group opposed it too. Only after it dawned on the Republican leaders that all Democrats and even some Republicans would not vote for it and that all the polls at the time were indicating in no uncertain terms that the bill was highly unpopular with the general public, did they let the bill die a natural death.

An analysis from the Congressional Budget Office estimated that a replacement would see premiums rising by 10 percent and would see 13 million fewer people insured after ten years, a scary scenario per se. The fact that a full repeal of "Obamacare" eluded Donald Trump and the Republicans in 2017 did not mean that they gave up the idea of fighting it.

One could say that 2018 ended with Donald Trump and the Republicans in Congress applauding themselves for their success in passing a massive tax bill that weakens the Affordable Care Act a little because effective 2019, the sweeping tax reforms repeal the penalty on people who choose not to buy health insurance, even though they might be able to afford it. Even though the individual mandate, as it is known, is considered a pillar of Obamacare, it was considered one of the least popular provisions in the Affordable Care Act and it actually affects or affected a relatively small percentage of Americans.

However, when on March 25, 2018, the Trump administration made a request to a federal appeals court that the whole Affordable Care Act be abolished; they inadvertently set the stage for another clash between the executive on the one hand and those in the different arms of government and the public on the other, who do not want a repeal of "Obamacare". At a time that the House of Representatives has a Democratic majority that is headed by a no-nonsense Nancy Pelosi who considers the passing of "Obamacare" to be one of her biggest political achievements during her years as the Speaker of the United States House of Representatives and as the House Minority Leader, it is difficult to imagine that the reignited fight to repeal "Obamacare" would be an easy one for Donald Trump and the Republican Party.

XIII: Revamp NATO

Besides Donald Trump's previous statements during his election campaign questioning the relevance of NATO (the North Atlantic Treaty Organization), which is an international military alliance established on 4 April 1949 to counter the USRR and its satellite states in Eastern Europe at the onset of the Cold War, Donald Trump showed the world that he was serious about changes to NATO during a dedication ceremony at the new NATO headquarters in Brussels on May 25, 2017. He chose this particular occasion to criticize some of the leaders of the NATO member states for falling short on their financial contributions in 2016 by a combined total of $119 billion, money that he thought could have been used to finance additional tasks for the alliance, such as to combat "the threat of terrorism."

However, the US. President has since then allayed the fears of most of the alliance's member states over statements he made in the past when he repeatedly questioned the military alliance's purpose, to the point of even calling it "obsolete". He is actually strengthening US military ties with these countries in many aspects, contrary to his campaign promises.

A fundamental change in Donald Trump's attitude towards the alliance was seen when he hosted NATO Secretary-General Jens Stoltenberg at the White House in April 2017, during which he told the Norwegian that the threat of terrorism had underlined the alliance's importance. *"I said it [NATO] was obsolete,"* Donald Trump said. *"It's no longer obsolete."*

The fact that Donald Trump is no longer fretting about the failure of most of the North Atlantic Treaty Organization's 28 member countries in their obligation to meet the alliance's goal of spending at least 2% of their gross domestic product on defense by 2024, indicates the extent of his change of heart on NATO. Still, his prodding stance on those NATO members that have a lackluster attitude towards meeting their obligations to the defense alliance has been welcomed in many quarters, especially by those who were also becoming worried about NATO's declining *raison d'être.*

NATO was gripped by a revived sense of purpose in February 2014 following Ukraine's tilt towards the West as a result of the Western-backed overthrow of the pro-Russian fourth Ukrainian president Viktor Yanukovych in what is called the Ukrainian revolution of 2014, and also known in some circles as the Euromaidan Revolution or Revolution of Dignity. This violent change of power sparked reactions from pro-Russian forces in Ukraine and from Russia itself. Russia responded by orchestrating the annexation of Crimea—a move that Russia and the country's supporters at home and abroad refer to as Crimea's reintegration or vote of reunification with Russia; and anti-Euromaidan forces protested and resisted the unconstitutional change, resulting in the armed conflict in Ukraine's Donbass provinces of Donetsk and Lugansk, with the result that close to half of these territories that opposed the overthrow of their native son are now unrecognized People's Republics. This further decline in Ukraine/NATO relations with Russia into what some analysts consider a new Cold War, did not give the alliance the new lease of life that its hawks wanted until the rise to power of Donald Trump. As a matter of fact, in 2016, only five NATO member states (USA, UK, Greece, Estonia, and Poland) met the goal or target of 2% contribution of their GDP to defense.

It counted as a plus for NATO that Donald Trump's incessant drumbeat since the start of his presidency in 2017 for the alliance's members to pay more has yielded positive results, so that NATO member states are likely to meet the target of spending at least 2% of their gross domestic product on defense by 2024. This optimistic outlook is based on the fact that NATO's spending as a share of GDP rose from 1.42 percent in 2016 to 1.45 percent in 2017, and then to 1.47 percent in 2018. With the USA aside, in raw dollar terms, expenditures by NATO members increased from $286 billion in 2016 to $301 billion in 2017 to $312 billion in 2018.

This new reality of a NATO that is growing in strength, especially regarding the seriousness of the member countries to fulfill their ends of the bargain, is expected to continue beyond 2018, an upswing that is attributed to Donald Trump's tough stance on NATO members who had been failing to meet their financial obligations to the defense organization. Even so, many geo-strategists think the fading possibility of an immediate resolution to the Ukraine Conflict that some describe as a tug-of-war between Russia and the West, owes a lot to Donald Trump's strengthening of the NATO alliance and America's deteriorating relations with Russia.

Still, advocates for global peace and those concerned with the advancement of unity and integration between the nations of Europe and Eurasia hope Donald's Trump's campaign promise to improve relations with Russia would make the existence of NATO irrelevant. Many of them see a fruitful Trump-Putin understanding followed by agreements on a wide range of issues as the only way forward to set both nations on the path of better cooperation or as the only practical form of reset.

Exponents of a US-Russian rapprochement count on the Mueller Report's absolution of Donald Trump of Collusion with Russia as the first step in a long and difficult journey to unhinge the sanctions imposed on Russia since the

Ukraine debacle, in order to create a new reality where the United States of America and Russia would-be allies, and NATO would have outlived its cold-war purpose. In this regard, the rise to power in Ukraine of civic-nationalist forces that did not participate in the country's acrimonious politics until their 2019 victories in the country's March/May presidential elections and its July parliamentary election, as well as the electoral disgrace suffered by the corrupt and nationalistic pro-Western forces that rose to power in 2014 following the overthrow of Ukraine's fourth president Yanukovych, contributing in making the grounds fertile for reconciliation between Russia and Ukraine, as well as for a reset in Russia-US/NATO relations.

XIII: Ban on Lobbying

Back in 2016, most of those with a desire to see "clean politics" practiced in the USA and who at the same understood the nature of lobbying, could hardly fault Donald Trump for his campaign promise to place a 5-year ban on lobbying, an undertaking that would involve the reinstitution of a ban for five years on all congressional and executive branch officials to prevent them from seeking to influence the government during that time frame after they leave the government or stop working for any of its branches. This pledge to "drain the swamp" of Washington by enacting new ethics laws, was expected to rattle the political establishment's way of doing business in a fairly significant manner. Donald Trump was supposed to ask Congress to pass this ban into law so that it cannot be lifted by executive order.

This pledge arose from the degenerating nature of the policy that first came into effect in 2007 following the Honest Leadership and Open Government Act that gave senators a two-year cooling-off period and House representatives a one-year period after they leave government, before they could start lobbying their former offices or committees for the sake of other groups, individuals, businesses and governments.

What we see 800-plus days into the Trump presidency are what his supporters call tentative steps towards the ban on lobbying, but what his detractors call ineptitude or renegation in that aspect of ethics reforms. The 45th president's January 28, 2017, executive order on lobbying, though better than Barack Obama's and Bill Clinton's, fell short because it only restricts some of the lobbying activities of White House officials after they leave his team, while it places no restrictions on members of Congress. In fact, 48.8 percent (80) of the 164 members of the 113th Congress who sought jobs after the 2014 midterm elections are currently employed at lobbying firms.

The fact that the president only signed an executive order instead of getting Congress to pass it into law and the fact that this order did not do much besides restricting some of the lobbyings that executive branch officials can do attest to the deep contrast between the actions taken and the promise made. All the same, most pundits agree that the president kept his promise on this one, even though it came across as a compromise.

XIV: Termination of Obama's Immigration Executive orders

Donald Trump's campaign promise on the issue of immigration read thus:

> *"Immediately terminate President Obama's two illegal executive amnesties (Deferred Action for Parents of Americans and Lawful Permanent Residents and Deferred Action for Childhood Arrivals). All immigration laws will be enforced -- we will triple the number of ICE agents. Anyone who enters the U.S. illegally is subject to deportation. That is what it means to have laws and to have a country."*

The deportation of criminal undocumented immigrants and the cancellation of some visas was a Trump promise that warmed him into the hearts of those opposed to immigration or unregulated movement of foreigners into the USA, as some of his supporters would like to call it. His post-election stance to deport some two to three million people who "are criminals and have criminal records, gang members, drug dealers..." is a far cry from his early campaign pledge to deport all 11.3 million undocumented immigrants in the country.

The US-based think tank The Migration Policy Institute

puts the figure of illegal immigrants with criminal records at 890,000. It is too early to determine the success or failure of this particular promise made by Donald Trump.

The two-and-a-half-year-old Trump administration has put on hold its promise to cancel visas to foreign countries that won't take back its citizens deported from the USA. However, the immigration enforcement priorities of the Trump Administration have resulted in the revival of deportation orders that the Obama administration ignored. This is buttressed by statistics showing that illegal border crossings have been declining since 2016. In fact, an April 2017 report from the Washington Post showed that arrests of immigrants without criminal records by the Immigration and Customs Enforcement (UCE) has more than doubled when compared to the previous year, a trend that has not relented since.

Today, the current administration can credit itself for successfully rescinding the controversial deportation-reprieve program for parents, which is a 2012 Obama-era memo that created Deferred Action for Parents of Americans and Lawful Permanent Residents, better known as DAPA. However he has experienced noteworthy setbacks in his efforts to get rid of the Deferred Action for Childhood Arrivals, or DACA, a still Obama-era program that began on June 15, 2012, and that is credited for preventing the deportation of some young immigrants who were brought into the country as children and who happened to be in the USA unlawfully. DACA ensures their continuous stay in the USA by allowing them to receive a renewable two-year period of deferred action from deportation and by making them eligible for a work permit in the USA.

XV: Stop the Funding of Sanctuary Cities

Donald Trump's pledge to cancel federal funding to "sanctuary cities" (these are American cities and counties that made it a policy to limit their cooperation with the national government and the US. Immigration and Customs Enforcement in the enforcement of immigration laws so as to reduce the fear of deportation and possible family break-up among people who are in the country illegally, thereby encouraging these susceptible immigrants to be more willing to report crimes, use health and social services, and enroll their children in school) was expected to draw a great deal of controversy. And it sure did. For a starter, he made the promise on the grounds that illegal immigrants pose a threat to public safety in the country, even though numerous studies have proven that native-born Americans are more inclined to commit crimes than immigrants, regardless of their legal status.

There are over 500 of these sanctuary settlements (cities and counties). Before the elections, especially during the period of campaigning from 2015-2016, Donald Trump thought it would be an easy promise to fulfill since Republicans were the majority in both houses of Congress, and since the Republican senator from Pennsylvania Pat Toomey had introduced in June 2016 a similar bill in the

Senate called "Stop Dangerous Sanctuary Cities Act", aimed at blocking sanctuary jurisdictions from getting grants under certain economic and community development programs. Even though the bill failed to advance, it gave Donald Trump some hope and a sense of direction on how to go about the matter.

So when in late April 2017, the new president came up with an executive order targeting the leaders of the so-called sanctuary cities by threatening to revoke federal funding over their failure to cooperate with immigration officials, it marked a real seriousness in Donald Trump's bid to honor that pledge in his list of campaign promises. However, a judge in San Francisco blocked the executive order, a move that since then has been serving as a harbinger of things to come because other legal actions took place afterward that blocked the Trump administration from fulfilling that campaign promise. That is why the so-called sanctuary cities have continued receiving federal funding.

To get around the impasse, the Trump administration is working on a narrow redefinition of "sanctuary cities", and has even suggested to mayors that the action would not affect many cities, thereby dangling the possibility that they would not be affected.

XVI: Nominate a Supreme Court Judge Replacement

The nomination of a Supreme Court judge was one of the promises Donald Trump made as a Republican Party nominee. He accomplished the task in January 2017 by nominating the conservative Judge Neil Gorsuch who is widely seen as qualified for the job to fill the Supreme Court seat left vacant on February 13, 2016, by the late Antonin Scalia following his untimely death.

Donald Trump encapsulated the views of many in the upper echelons of both the Republican Party and the Democratic party when he said of Neil Gorsuch on Jan. 31, 2017 that:

"I took the task of this nomination very seriously. I've selected an individual whose qualities define—really, and I mean closely define—what we're looking for. Judge Gorsuch has outstanding legal skills, a brilliant mind, tremendous discipline and has earned bipartisan support."

As a matter of fact, besides standing out from Donald Trump's initial list of 20 judges, Neil Gorsuch made history when on April 10, 2017, at age 49, he became the youngest Associate Justice of the Supreme Court of the United States since Clarence Thomas, who was appointed supreme court judge by George H.W. Bush in 1991 at the age of 43. As a result, he displaced Chief Justice John Roberts (in office since September 29, 2005) and Justice Elena Kagan (in office since August 7, 2010) who were both 50 years old when they became Supreme Court judges.

XVII: Achieve Complete Energy Independence

One of Donald Trump's catching campaign promises is contained in his "An America First Energy Plan," where he pledged to promote American energy self-sufficiency by lifting *"the Obama-Clinton roadblocks and allowing vital energy infrastructure projects, like the Keystone Pipeline, to move forward."* This pledge was against the backdrop of the fact that improvements had been made in this regard under the last three presidencies to the point where domestic energy production in 2017 met about 90% of U.S. energy consumption, a trend that could meet Donald Trump's energy goal to make the USA a self-sufficient country in energy production by the end of his presidency, thereby circumventing US. foes and the oil cartels from using energy as a weapon against the United States of America.

A table on Net Generation by Energy Source from 2009-2018 in Thousand Megawatt-hours reveals the following:

Generation at Utility-Scale Facilities						
Period	Coal	Petroleum Liquids	Petroleum Coke	Natural Gas	Other Gas	Nuclear
Annual Totals						
2009	1,755,904	25,972	12,964	920,979	10,632	798,855
2010	1,847,290	23,337	13,724	987,697	11,313	806,968
2011	1,733,430	16,086	14,096	1,013,689	11,566	790,204
2012	1,514,043	13,403	9,787	1,225,894	11,898	769,331
2013	1,581,115	13,820	13,344	1,124,836	12,853	789,016

2014	1,581,710	18,276	11,955	1,126,609	12,022	797,166
2015	1,352,398	17,372	10,877	1,333,482	13,117	797,178
2016	1,239,149	13,008	11,197	1,378,307	12,807	805,694
2017	1,205,835	12,414	8,976	1,296,415	12,469	804,950
2018	1,146,393	15,742	8,830	1,468,013	12,191	807,078

	Generation at Utility-Scale Facilities					
Period	Hydro-electric	Solar	Renewable Sources Excluding Hydro-electric and Solar	Hydro-electric Pumped Storage	Other	Total Generation at Utility-Scale Facilities
	Annual Totals					
2009	273,445	891	143,388	-4,627	11,928	3,950,331
2010	260,203	1,212	165,961	-5,501	12,855	4,125,060
2011	319,355	1,818	192,163	-6,421	14,154	4,100,141
2012	276,240	4,327	214,006	-4,950	13,787	4,047,765
2013	268,565	9,036	244,472	-4,681	13,588	4,065,964
2014	259,367	17,691	261,522	-6,174	13,461	4,093,606
2015	249,080	24,893	270,268	-5,091	14,028	4,077,601
2016	267,812	36,054	305,579	-6,686	13,754	4,076,675
2017	300,333	53,286	332,991	-6,495	13,094	4,034,268
2018	291,724	66,604	354,445	-5,905	12,695	4,177,810

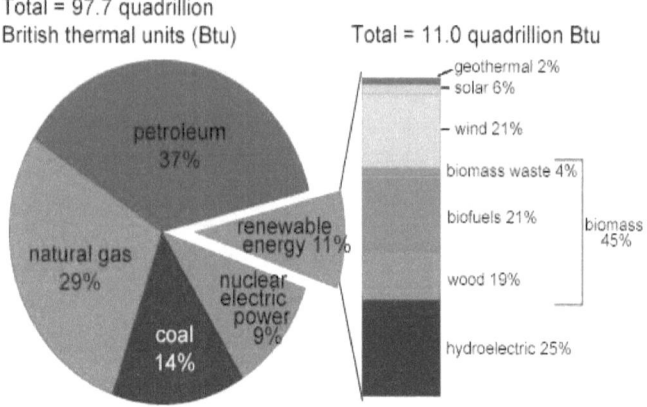

U.S. energy consumption by energy source, 2017

Total = 97.7 quadrillion
British thermal units (Btu)   Total = 11.0 quadrillion Btu

petroleum
37%

natural gas
29%

renewable
energy 11%

nuclear
electric
power
9%

coal
14%

geothermal 2%
solar 6%
wind 21%
biomass waste 4%
biofuels 21%
wood 19%
hydroelectric 25%

biomass
45%

Note. Sum of components may not equal 100% because of independent rounding.
Source: U.S. Energy Information Administration, *Monthly Energy Review*, Table 1.3
and 10.1, April 2018, preliminary data   eia

Donald Trump's game plan to achieve that energy self-sufficiency is centered on ensuring the resumption of stalled Obama-era energy infrastructure projects like the Dakota-Access and Keystone pipelines, as well as on encouraging the pursuit of new ones. It has sparked off criticism from opponents who hold that his focus is disproportionately on the production of fossil fuels or primary sources of energy (petroleum, natural gas, and coal) at a time that some of America's allies and competitors are investing more on nuclear energy (nuclear power plants) and renewable sources of energy that make use of sunlight, wind, rain, tides, waves, and geothermal heat. The rapid deployment of these non-primary sources of energy and their use of energy efficiency technologies is bringing about significant energy security for many countries, climate change mitigation, and economic benefits for their governments and the people.

XVIII: Reverse Barack Obama's Executive Actions

Donald Trump's promise to reverse Obama executive actions did not come as a surprise to many of those versed with the actions of past presidents since most new presidents replace the administration of their predecessors, especially those from rival political parties, promising to overturn the reversible policies of the outgoing presidents. Such actions are usually meant as a statement of loyalty to their own parties. The president has had mixed results in this regard so far. Several Obama orders, like gun control regulations that the right-wing National Rifle Association (NRA) opposes, have been undone, but the Trump administration hasn't taken actions on several others such as the Department of Education's guidelines on the public-school bathrooms that transgender children should use.

XIX: Cancel Payments to the UNO on "Global Warming"

The cancellation of billions in *"...payments to U.N. climate change programs, and using the money instead to fix America's water and environmental infrastructure."* is one of Donald Trump's pre-election pledges regarding the controversial subject of climate change. As president, his efforts to keep this promise have produced mixed results. He has even asked Congress to stop funding the programs as evidenced by his 2017 proposed budget demanding that the United States ceased funding the Climate Change Initiative and the United Nation's Green Climate Fund. Of particular note is his reason, holding that money from this fund *"will be sent to the very countries and factories that have taken our jobs."*

However, all was not lost for those who take climate change seriously because, on Sept. 7, 2017, the Senate Appropriations Committee approved an amendment that not only restored full U.S. funding for the United Nations Framework Convention on Climate but that also fully restored funding for the Intergovernmental Panel on Climate Change. Democratic Party Senator Jeff Merkley of Oregon who sponsored the amendment claimed that it brought "…*funding levels in line with recent U.S. support for those institutions…"* in the United Nations.

XX: Encourage School Choice

"School choice" is a term for K–12 public education options covering a variety of programs and laws providing public funding to K-12 students and their families that allows them alternatives to schools that are publicly funded (magnet and charter schools, inter- and intra-district transfers, and traditional neighborhood schools) or schools that are not within the public system (private schools, vouchers and tax credits, homeschooling) other than the neighborhood school that is generally assigned to them based on the residential boundary lines of their families.

The promotion of School Choice laws and programs nationwide and the Expansion of Education was a promise Donald Trump kept repeating right up to election day. One statement he made in this regard which clearly stood out was his pledge to *"Immediately add an additional federal investment of $20 billion towards school choice."* However, as president, Donald Trump has encountered roadblocks in his efforts to redirect *"education dollars to give parents the right to send their kids to the public, private, charter, magnet, religious or home school of their choice,"* and expand vocational and technical education, improve two- and four-year college affordability, as well as end federal Common Core, which is s a state-led effort that is not part of "No Child Left Behind" or any other federal initiative.

When he asked Congress in 2017 to create a national school voucher program and to allot $1.4 billion toward school choice in the 2018 fiscal year budget, it was seen as a robust effort to fulfill this particular promise. But Congress has so far failed to comply, besides a token $28 million increase in charter school spending in 2018. With Betsy DeVos, the newly appointed education secretary, who also happens to be a school choice advocate, some progress is expected in this direction, even though Congress has been dragging its feet.

XXI: Creation of Targeted Child Care Tax Credits

The promise Donald Trump made as the Republican nominee to work on improving Child Care Law was not explicit enough. Even though there are references in the outline of the tax reform plan about "providing tax relief for families with child and dependent care expenses", and even though members of the Trump administration have met with lawmakers and others to discuss the issue of childcare and paid leave, their scope pale in comparison to Donald Trump's pre-election promise of a bill that *"allows Americans to deduct childcare and eldercare from their taxes, incentivizes employers to provide on-site childcare services and creates tax-free dependent care savings accounts for both young and elderly dependents, with matching contributions for low-income families."*

As it currently stands, no stand-alone childcare legislation has been proposed by the Trump administration and the December 2017 tax bill failed to directly address the issue, even though there were changes to tax credits, leaving both low-income and high-income families getting slightly more than they had been getting before, but far less than they would have been getting if Donald Trump had fulfilled this particular campaign promise.

XXII: Impose Term Limits on Members of Congress

The Trump administration has not had any breakthrough in

its efforts, in conjunction with the Republican Party, to fulfill his campaign promise regarding a constitutional amendment to impose term limits on all members of Congress. This is so despite the fact that a variety of Republican lawmakers had, by March 2017, introduced eight bills to impose term limits in the House of Representatives. Ted Cruz who had a tough run against Donald Trump in the Republican primaries also introduced a bill on term limits in the Senate, where Mitch McConnell, the Senate Majority Leader who himself is a Republican, dominates. And strangely enough, Mitch McConnell is against the idea of term limits, convinced that elections take care of that, based on his statement that: *"I would say we have term limits now. They're called elections. And it will not be on the agenda in the Senate."*

XXIII: Increase Health Care of Veterans

Donald Trump's election promise to pass a law without delay that would allow veterans to "receive public VA (Veterans Affairs) treatment or attend the private doctor of their choice," came to fruition with the signing of two bills into law in April 2017—one extending a program giving some veterans the option to get medical care from private doctors, and the other enhancing whistleblower protections at the VA that guarantee their freedom of speech.

The 2018 budget called for an overall increase of 3.5 percent for the VA department, as well as a 6 percent hike for its medical programs, a clear enough indication that the Trump administration would continue in its efforts to improve the quality of life of the veterans and reduce the ineligibility rate.

XXIV: Bomb the Islamic State into Oblivion

Perhaps the most flashy or sensational of all the campaign promises that Donald Trump made in his bid to become the 45th president of the United States of America, and which he has fulfilled involves the April 13, 2017 dropping of the biggest non-nuclear bomb in the arsenal of the United States military on an IS-stronghold—the Khorasan cave complex in the Achin District, in the Nangarhar Province, in Afghanistan. The use of the GBU-43/B Massive Ordnance Air Blast (MOAB), dubbed the "Mother of All Bombs" is regarded by most Trump supporters as the total and complete fulfillment of his November 2015 promise made during a speech in Iowa to bomb the Islamic State (ISIS) into oblivion.

When Donald Trump stated on March 23, 2019 that, *"I am pleased to announce that, together with our partners in the Global Coalition to defeat ISIS, including the Iraqi Security Forces and the Syrian Democratic Forces, the United States has liberated all ISIS-controlled territories in Syria and Iraq —100 percent of the caliphate,"* he basically touched on a promise that got fulfilled with the cooperation of some, but not all of the forces involved in the fight against ISIS in that part of the Middle East.

XXV: Take Home No Salary

When before the election, Donald Trump said that *"If I'm elected president, I'm accepting no salary,"* his statement raised many eyebrows. Words like those coming from a businessman are unusual. However, as the 45th US. President of the USA, he has so far kept his promise by donating what he earned to different entities. As the information below shows:

- Between January 20 and March 31, 2017, he donated the pre-tax amount of $78,333, to the National Park Service
- He gifted his 2017 second quarterly paychecks to the Department of Education
- The 45th president's donation of all of his third-quarter presidential salary went to the Department of Health and Human Services as a contribution to its efforts to combat the opioid crisis.
- The Transportation Department got the 2017 fourth quarter paychecks
- The president's 2018 first quarter paychecks went to the Veterans Administration
- The Small Business Administration was the recipient of the president's 2018 second quarter paychecks

- Donald Trump's 2018 Third-Quarter Salary went to an Organization that funds Alcoholism Research
- The president's fourth-quarter 2018 paychecks went to the Department of Transportation
- The Department of Homeland Security got the president's 2019 first quarter paychecks

As things stand, Donald Trump has been honoring his promise not to take a paycheck. So, unless he stops making a donation of his quarterly paychecks, we can say that this is one promise he has fulfilled one hundred percent.

XXVI: Create a Private White House Veterans Hotline

Many people did not take Donald Trump seriously when he said during his quest to become the 45th president of the United States of America that, *"I will create a private White House hotline – that is answered by a real person 24 hours a day – to make sure that no valid complaint about the VA ever falls through the cracks. I will instruct my staff that if a valid complaint is not acted upon, then the issue be brought directly to me, and I will pick up the phone and fix it myself, if need be."*. However, he created a White House Veterans Hotline all right, tasked with helping at-crisis risk Veterans needing the services of the Veterans Crisis Line. This service is linked with the VA (Veterans Affairs).

White House Veterans Hotline is explicitly tasked with answering inquiries, providing directory assistance, documenting concerns about VA care, benefits and services; and with expediting the referral and solution of concerns. He fulfilled that promise in mid-October 2017, and today, about 200,000 calls have been handled by its staff.

XXVII: Miscellaneous

Exhaustive that the promises Donald Trump made to the electorate were, the above mentioned were the catchiest, according to most pundits. However, other promises or vows that Donald Trump made are capable of having a great impact on the socio-economic and even political landscape of the country.

Donald Trump has issued a lot of executive orders during the first 800 days of his presidency, and most of them were not challenged, unlike the case with the so-called "Muslim Ban". Some of the unchallenged executive orders include among others:

- The creation of a task force aimed at reducing surging crime, drugs and violence and increasing funding for programs that train and assist local police
- A federal hiring freeze that excluded military personnel and public safety personnel. However, he lifted the hiring freeze in April 2017.
- The promise to cut two federal regulations for every new one, which he set about accomplishing in January 2017 with a signed executive action

ordering federal agencies to "identify at least two existing regulations to be repealed", meaning to be replaced by every new one proposed.

The 45th American president is also working in tandem with Congress on some of his promises, such as establishing new mandatory minimum sentences for immigration crimes, increasing resources to federal law enforcement and prosecutors in the effort to "dismantle criminal gangs and put violent offenders behind bars."

Besides the above, Donald Trump also promised to carry out within the first 100 days of his presidency a host of other changes that included:

- A revenue-neutral infrastructure package that would leverage "public-private partnerships, and private investments through tax incentives to spur $1 trillion in infrastructure investment over ten years". The president promised to invest $550 billion in infrastructure and create an infrastructure fund when he said, above other things that *"The Trump Administration seeks to invest $550 billion to ensure we can export our goods and move our people faster and safer."* The promise has so far stalled as even the last proposal he made in February 2018 to inject $200 billion in hard federal dollars into infrastructure, a far cry from the cited half-trillion figure, failed to gain traction. With the Democrats in control of the House of Representatives after their gains in the 2018 midterm elections resulted in a split Congress, it is now hard to imagine how would be possible for the Trump administration to find a consensus with the Democrats on this promise. The top Senate Democrat Chuck Schumer of New York, highlighted the bumpy road ahead when he made it known to Donald Trump that he should expect no deal on infrastructure unless the president made a substantial investment in the campaign to combat climate change. The fact that most Republicans do not consider climate change a man-made phenomenon makes a deal hinged on such a consensus far-fetched, hence a hard sell

- Putting an end to defense sequester, which appears to be ambiguous at best or faltering at worst, particularly due to the fact that the Trump budget requested more defense spending

- Coming up with a Cybersecurity plan. So, far, no steps have been taken by the Trump administration on his promise of a Cybersecurity plan even after hosting a group in the White House in late January 2017 to discuss it

- Taking steps to change the name of the highest mountain peak in North America, from Mount Denali back to Mount McKinley which is how it was officially called from 1917 until 2015, even though the native Koyukon people of Alaska who have been inhabiting the area around the mountain for centuries always referred to the peak as "Denali". No steps have been taken to fulfill that promise, and it is unlikely that Donald Trump would try to fulfill it. So it is considered broken. The reason stems from the fact that when in March 2017, the president met with Republican Senators from Alaska —Lisa Murkowski and Dan Sullivan —they told him that they and most of their constituents would oppose the move because the name of the mountain was conferred by the Athabascan people more than 10,000 years ago.

- Adopting The 'Penny Plan' which *"...would reduce non-defense, non-safety net spending by one percent of the previous year's total each year. Over 10 years, the plan will reduce spending (outlays) by almost $1 trillion without touching defense or entitlement spending..."* So far, the Trump Administration has not fulfilled that promise and Congress is yet to find a place in its budget for any plan on it.

- Et cetera.

CHAPTER FOUR

The Hand of Cooperation

"Sometimes people don't want to hear the truth because they don't want their illusions destroyed."
Friedrich Nietzsche

"It is the mark of an educated mind to be able to entertain a thought without accepting it."
Aristotle

If you take a walk or a drive down the street of any town or city in the United States of America or down the road of any settlement in the countryside, and then stop and randomly ask the people what they think of the first two and a half years of the Trump presidency, do not be surprised to find that more than five out of every ten American thinks the 45th US. President's time in office has been melodramatic in one form or the other. This falls in line with the results of research and the conclusions of respectable analysts and thinkers that all point to the fact that even though the heightened emotions that have characterized the Trump presidency since 2017 reached an unusually unhealthy level, the degree of dichotomy and hostilities was exaggerated by a wide range of interest groups in the country, of which the most prominent have been politicians of all stripes, Trump opponents, the media and the bureaucracy, as well as Donald Trump and his retinue.

When the president told a group of Coast Guard graduates on May 17, 2017, that *"Look at the way I've been treated lately, especially by the media...No politician in history, and I say this with great surety, has been treated worse or more unfairly...",* his words carried a lot of truth in them, though not the whole truth because he fuelled if not triggered the media's anti-Trump hysteria to some extent, even if he did so unconsciously.

The above statement belies an underlying reality. The president in a subtle way wishes that the state of affairs in the country could be different. For a man who is viewed by many Americans as someone who became the president by riding roughshod over his opponents in the Republican primaries, for a man who stunned most Americans and the rest of the world by pulling off an upset win against his

Democratic rival Hilary Clinton, his statements deploring "unfair" treatment could be construed as an attempt or even a conscious effort to stir the conscience of those who are against him, garner sympathy from those who are for and against him, as well as shore up his support base. But then, there could be another side to the president's objection to the way he is being treated by his opponents. Maybe Donald Trump is seeking a truce. Or maybe he even wants peace and reconciliation between the different socio-economic and political factions in the USA for the sake of a united front in tackling America's domestic and foreign challenges.

Some Trump supporters strongly hold that he wants to work with everyone to get things done, to "Make America Great Again" as he promised during the campaigns. A faction of them even points to his May 13, 2017 statement from the podium at Liberty University where he said among other things that *"Nothing is easier and more pathetic than being a critic, because they're people that can't get the job done."* That statement and similar others beg the question:

Has the president, over the last two and a half years, been vigorous enough in his efforts to implement his campaign promises?

One would be belittling the obvious by stating again that a lot has happened since Donald Trump's inauguration on January 10, 2017, as the 45th president of the United States of America. As a matter of fact, the president's opponents have used all sorts of adjectives to describe his personality, character, and actions, words that in a nutshell portray him as an American version of Don Quixote. But however quixotic his naysayers portray him and his presidency, many of these same critics grudgingly admit that his drive to fulfill his promises has exceeded the expectations of most Americans. That does not mean there is no room for criticism even from Donald Trump's supporters and sympathizers. We see that the one thing virtually all the camps can agree on is the fact that the president has been good for the media business.

While some of the policy actions Donald Trump took exposed his inexperience, lack of knowledge and insensitivity, they nonetheless showed his resolve, and in some cases survival instincts. And though his resolve is something that irks his opponents a lot, it is a quality his supporters expected and have been expecting from him. After all, his pledge to *"Drain the Swamps"* entailed clobbering those responsible for the rut in the management of the country; and it entailed knocking some sense into the heads of those who are happy or are comfortable with the status quo. And confronting the elites of the country's entrenched political class, business groups and military-industrial complex with interests to defend is something that only a man of mettle can endeavor, especially in a country with an established system that has never seen an overhaul or that has never experienced radical changes.

But then, in a presidency that has so far been full of drama, in a Trump administration that is indeed expected to continue being sensational, grit alone is not enough. So, it would be foolhardy to expect or to say that the rest of Donald Trump's term(s) in office is going to be a failure as his detractors wish, or that it is going to be splendid as those who are rooting for him are praying for or imagine it would be. Many forces are at play here. That is why pundits are split when it comes to whether he has what it takes to be the ultimate pace-setter of his presidency. Conflicting though the views regarding the nature of his presidency are, one thing for sure is that if he must serve the four years of his presidency and win another term in office, then he would have to engage in some skillful politics.

Brinksmanship is an art most politicians not fettered by ideology rarely practice. So it was not expected from a businessman and media personality like Donald Trump whose record of political loyalty was questionable. After all, he identified himself as a Republican for several years until August 2001, the year he first changed his party affiliation. But that was not even all about it. After abandoning the party of Ronald Reagan, he went on to identify himself as a Democrat for eight years until September 2009 when he switched sides again and rejoined the Republican party. Donald Trump became an independent (no party affiliation) in December 2011, stayed as one for four months, only to once again return to the Republican party where he used his party membership this time around to run in its primaries for the 2016 presidential election, which he won, before emerging victorious in the race itself to become the United States of America's current president.

When Donald Trump folded his sleeves right after he got into the White House and started acting on virtually all the core promises he made during the 2015/2016 primaries and the election campaign, he sent a strong message to those who voted for him and those who did not that he was a man of his words, a move that has achieved the remarkable result of solidifying his support base. So the shutdown that lasted for 35 days, from December 22, 2018 until January 25, 2019, which is a classic case of brinksmanship, showed an underlying conviction behind the president's attempt to fulfill his promise to build the U.S.–Mexico border wall, as well as his resolve to overcome the impasse in Congress where Democrats did not want to approve the $5.7 billion in federal funds that he was demanding for the border wall's construction.

Analysts were quick to see the lack of an ideological content in the president's conviction, especially since the shutdown indirectly cost the American economy an estimated $11 billion, and since several opinion polls showed that the percentage of Americans who held him responsible for the shutdown was higher than the proportion that put the blame on Democrats. As a matter of fact, the differences in the percentages are in their double digits.

Even before Donald Trump's inauguration, analysts worth their salt knew that ideologically-driven and/or "rational minds" in the other branches of the government of the United States of America (the Judiciary and the Legislative) would not allow the new president to do whatever he wanted to do, such as the use of his executive orders to prevent non-Americans from entering the USA because of their religion, on difficult to defend grounds that the measures are aimed at stopping terrorism, especially since a country like Saudi Arabia that produced most of the foreign terrorists that attacked the United States on September 11, 2001, did not feature on the list. That among other things explains why the president has not yet taken steps to fulfill all of his pre-election promises. That is why it would be fair to say that even though he has not carried out many of the promises he set out to fulfill, he cannot be accused of not trying.

So, who is to blame for Donald Trump's failure to be an A or an A+ president as even his supporters would say, or for being a B or a B+ president as many fair-minded analysts think, or even for being an underachiever or a failing president as his unwavering critics or opponents hold?

It does not need a guru to tell anyone that Donald Trump, his administration and even his supporters are critical of the political establishment in the country. It is obvious they also blame the media. As a matter of fact, some Trump supporters also blame the Republican Party, especially its elites, by citing as an example their much-talked-about promise to replace "Obamacare", a promise that fell apart after their first attempt to do away with the program, and which since then seems not to be going anywhere. Some of the "Trumpists" view the abortive replacement as the desire of the Republican elites to sabotage his presidency.

Donald Trump on his part can blame the Democratic Party for failing to work with him; he can blame the unelected bureaucracy for working against his plans and undermining his authority; and he can even harp on the multinational corporations too for not cooperating with him the way he wants in his effort to "Bring Manufacturing Back" to the United States of America.

At this stage of the Trump presidency, it would be injudicious to heap the entire blame on anyone or on a particular group for some of the impasses in the country, or for the gridlock as some would say. Pundits who take Donald Trump and his opponents seriously acknowledge the fact that the grounds have not been fully tested, with both the pro-Trump and anti-Trump camps holding aces that they can use against one another whenever they deem it necessary. Nevertheless, looming ahead are either battles between the opposing forces or inevitable cooperation between the so-called antagonistic political ideologies and groups in the USA. The ferocity or blandness of those battles would largely be determined by the perception the different sides have of each other's strengths and/or weaknesses.

And whether we like him or hate him for his actions or as a person, Donald Trump has been fighting back in a tactical manner that is worthy of praise. He has been disarraying his opponents even further, intriguing and galvanizing his supporters in turns, and weakening the resolve of those with doubts about throwing in their lot with him. In fact, we see that the number of thinkers who cannot say for sure whether he is for capitalism, socialism or even democracy, is increasing every day.

How has the 45th president of the United States of America managed to reduce the once fearsome potential of the political establishment and the military-industrial complex, especially in their ability to influence and determine the policies of presidential administrations?

That is a question some detractors have asked in one form or the other. It doesn't need a political guru to explain the intriguing nature of the relationship between the Trump administration and the political establishment/military-industrial complex. The 45th president of the USA has been useful and detrimental in turns to the overall objectives and the grand strategy of these groups. In fact, some of their big guns are still convinced Donald Trump could be mellowed to become their useful tool at the end of the day by enhancing their project that would see the United States of America maintaining its position as the world's only superpower and the leading force of globalism and globalization.

It is difficult to imagine that the president does not know about that grand design by a clique among the powers that be, especially the upholders of the "Wolfowitz Doctrine" that is considered imperialist in some circles. As a matter of fact, though written to form the final version of the Defense Planning Guidance for the 1994–99 fiscal years, many of its tenets are to be found in the "Bush Doctrine" that

Senator Edward M. Kennedy lucidly described as *"a call for 21st century American imperialism that no other nation can or should accept."* With many contours of which unilateralism and the use of preventative war are the most pronounced, one can easily see that the Bush Doctrine is still alive and strong in the corridors of power in Washington DC and that it is the fulcrum of American foreign and defense planning.

We don't have to go far back to see that Donald Trump's ability if not his willingness to challenge the status quo in Washington DC first came to the limelight with the way he began pushing back against the mainstream media, which is an indispensable tool in the hands of the powers that be. And he has been very skillful about it, improving as time goes by. In fact, one did not have to read between the lines to discern the skillful manner with which he took the media off his back on April 14, 2018, when he gave the orders for the Military of the United States of America to carry out multiple strikes, involving aircraft and ship-based missiles, against several Syrian government sites in the Arab country, thereby attracting the ire of the very same Russia that his political opponents and the elite media had been accusing him of fancying since the start of his presidency.

However, even by acting as a gung-ho commander-in-chief for a day only, even by appearing to be in line with the national security establishment which had been breathing down his neck since he made it to the Oval Office, he still failed to kill the story hanging over his head based on allegations made by his opponents even before his inauguration, that he colluded with Russia in order to win the 2016 presidential election, thereby casting him in the eyes of some as a Manchurian candidate. His May 09, 2017 firing of the seventh FBI director James Comey fuelled the story even further to the point where on May 17, 2017, a US. counterintelligence investigation called Special Counsel Investigation, and also referred to as the Mueller probe, Mueller Investigation or the Russia Investigation, was launched to look for links or coordination between the Russian government and members of the Trump presidential campaign, as well as "...any matters that arose or may arise directly from the investigation..."

As a matter of fact, many prominent voices in the different U.S. intelligence agencies had concluded back in January 2017 that the Russian government interfered in the 2016 presidential election by hacking into the computer servers of the Democratic National Committee (DNC), as well as into the personal Gmail account of John Podesta, who at the time was Hillary Clinton's campaign chairman; and that they got their hands on damaging contents that they transferred over to WikiLeaks for publication; that the government of Russian disseminated fake news by promoting it on social media; and that the Russian government penetrated or tried to penetrate the election systems and databases of several states in the USA.

The vexed president thought there was no reason to launch the Special Counsel investigation headed by Robert Swan Mueller III, the sixth Director of the Federal Bureau of Investigation (FBI), from 2001 to 2013. And many Americans thought so too, convinced that Donald Trump did not fire James Comey in order to kill an investigation into claims by his opponents that the Russians helped to get him elected in the 2016 presidential election. These skeptics, like Donald Trump, also thought James Comey was an unpredictable figure in the country's intelligence. After all, he was known to have been a registered Republican for most of his life until 2016, and was a man the Democrats accused of jeopardizing Hillary Clinton's expected win in the 2016 presidential election by his October 28, 2016 letter to members of Congress, advising them that the FBI was reviewing more of Hillary Clinton's emails. That piece of information, as it turned out, was leaked to the public shortly after by some Congressmen, thereby creating more doubts in the minds of those voters who were already wary about Hillary Clinton's trustworthiness as a future president. So, the fact that the Mueller Report, which was finally submitted to Attorney General William Barr on March 22, 2019, proved there was no collusion with Russia, one can say that Donald Trump is vindicated. But that was not all about the ripple effects of the investigation. It also underscored a major victory for Donald Trump in his struggle against his opponents in the national security establishment and the objectors among his political advisers.

Was Donald Trump actually looking forward to working with the political establishment of career Democrats and Republicans, the state bureaucracy, the corporate media and the military-industrial complex after he assumed office, even though he had promised "...to Drain the Swamp...", which is a description of his plan to fix problems in the federal government?

It would be tough to convince the average Democrat that the 45th president of the United States of America had consensus in mind during his inauguration or the days or weeks after he assumed office, when the platform of his campaign was built on the different shades of his notorious promises to *"Root Out Corruption"* in Washington and *"Make America Great Again"*. In fact, advocates for an uncompromising Donald Trump vis-à-vis the-powers-that-be find comfort in the fact that most of those who voted him to power expected him to be their perfect "human Molotov cocktail", as Michael Moore, the director of the American documentary film "Fahrenheit 9/11" pointed out in early November 2016. Voters, especially in the Rust Belt, were really upset with the system and used Donald Trump to send home that message by voting him to power, even though they did not agree with a lot of the things he said, and even though they doubted he could fulfill the myriads of promises he made during the long months of campaigning, even if he wanted to. After all, like the former FBI director James Comey that he fired shortly after he assumed office, Donald Trump too had shown his flexibility or ideological unreliability by affiliating in turns with the Republican Party, the Democratic Party and even with Independents. *Political Prostitution*, is what some Trump opponents attribute his past propensity to change political camps at will, to be.

"He can't be considered a political prostitute like most of those in Congress or the political establishment in general who happened to have been bought or sponsored by lobbyists, corporations, and interest groups, and because of that come across as prostitutes who have been paid for sexual favors. His actions were guided by free-will and his desire to find the right path. He can be accused of flip-flopping, even though I think he is a wise man who changes his mind." A Trump supporter once opined.

Trump supporters, detractors, and analysts unencumbered by the polarization in American politics only have to analyze Donald Trump's February 28, 2017 speech to Congress to get a feel of the balancing act his administration was hoping to pull off so as to avoid gridlock in running the country. Back then, they were well aware of the fact that in the coming days, weeks, months and years, the Democratic Party would do all within its powers to prevent the president from serving his full term of office, just like his predecessor Barack Obama encountered deadlock during his presidency while dealing with a House of Representatives and a Senate that were dominated by members of the Republican Party who in their overriding objective to make him a one-term president, made it their mission to thwart most of his initiatives to carry out reforms, most of which would have advanced the wellbeing of America and the average American. In this remarkable Joint Address to Congress, Donald Trump gave room for compromises that left many

Americans wondering what he really stood for. Was he sincere in his words or was he up to something else when he said the following among other things in the speech to the joint session:

"...Tonight, as we mark the conclusion of our celebration of Black History Month, we are reminded of our nation's path towards civil rights and the work that remains to be done. Recent threats targeting Jewish community centers and vandalism of Jewish cemeteries, as well as last week's shooting in Kansas City, remind us that while we may be a nation divided on policies, we are a country that stands united in condemning hate and evil in all of its very ugly forms.

Each American generation passes the torch of truth, liberty and justice in an unbroken chain all the way down to the present. That torch is now in our hands. And we will use it to light up the world. I am here tonight to deliver a message of unity and strength, and it is a message deeply delivered from my heart. A new chapter of American Greatness is now beginning. A new national pride is sweeping across our nation. And a new surge of optimism is placing impossible dreams firmly within our grasp.

What we are witnessing today is the renewal of the American spirit. Our allies will find that America is once again ready to lead. All the nations of the world -- friend or foe -- will find that America is strong, America is proud, and America is free.

In nine years, the United States will celebrate the 250th anniversary of our founding -- 250 years since the day we declared our independence. It will be one of the great milestones in the history of the world. But what will America look like as we reach our 250th year? What kind of country will we leave for our children?

For too long, we've watched our middle-class shrink as we've exported our jobs and wealth to foreign countries. We've financed and built one global project after another, but ignored the fates of our children in the inner cities of Chicago, Baltimore, Detroit, and so many other places throughout our land.

We've defended the borders of other nations while leaving our own borders wide open for anyone to cross and for drugs to pour in at a now unprecedented rate. And we've spent trillions and trillions of dollars overseas, while our infrastructure at home has so badly crumbled.

Then, in 2016, the Earth shifted beneath our feet. The rebellion started as a quiet protest, spoken by families of all colors and creeds -- families who just wanted a fair shot for their children and a fair hearing for their concerns.

But then the quiet voices became a loud chorus as thousands of citizens now spoke out together, from cities small and large, all across our country. Finally, the chorus became an earthquake, and the people turned out by the tens of millions, and they were all united by one very simple, but crucial demand: that America must put its own citizens first. Because only then can we truly make America great again.

Dying industries will come roaring back to life. Heroic veterans will get the care they so desperately need. Our military will be given the resources its brave warriors so richly deserve. Crumbling infrastructure will be replaced with new roads, bridges, tunnels, airports, and railways gleaming across our very, very beautiful land. Our terrible drug epidemic will slow down and, ultimately, stop. And our neglected inner cities will see a rebirth of hope, safety, and opportunity. Above all else, we will keep our promises to the American people.

It's been a little over a month since my inauguration, and I want to take this moment to update the nation on the progress I've made in keeping those promises.

Since my election, Ford, Fiat-Chrysler, General Motors, Sprint, Softbank, Lockheed, Intel, Wal-Mart, and many others have announced that they will invest billions and billions of dollars in the United States, and will create tens of thousands of new American jobs.

The stock market has gained almost $3 trillion in value since the election on November 8th, a record. We've saved taxpayers hundreds of millions of dollars by bringing down the price of a fantastic -- and it is a fantastic -- new F-35 jet fighter, and we'll be saving billions more on contracts all across our government. We have placed a hiring freeze on non-military and non-essential federal workers.

We have begun to drain the swamp of government corruption by imposing a five-year ban on lobbying by executive branch officials and a lifetime ban thank you -- and a lifetime ban on becoming lobbyists for a foreign government.

We have undertaken a historic effort to massively reduce job-crushing regulations, creating a deregulation task force inside of every government agency. And we're imposing a new rule which mandates that for everyone new regulation, two old regulations must be eliminated. We're going to stop the regulations that threaten the future and livelihood of our great coal miners.

We have cleared the way for the construction of the Keystone and Dakota Access Pipelines thereby creating tens of thousands of jobs. And I've issued a new directive that new American pipelines be made with American steel.

We have withdrawn the United States from the job-killing Trans-Pacific Partnership. And with the help of Prime Minister Justin Trudeau, we have formed a council with our neighbors in Canada to help ensure that women entrepreneurs have access to the networks, markets, and capital they need to start a business and live out their financial dreams.

To protect our citizens, I have directed the Department of Justice to form a Task Force on Reducing Violent Crime. I have further ordered the Departments of Homeland Security and Justice, along with the Department of State and the Director of National Intelligence, to coordinate an aggressive strategy to dismantle the criminal cartels that have spread all across our nation. We will stop the drugs from pouring into our country and poisoning our youth, and we will expand treatment for those who have become so badly addicted.

At the same time, my administration has answered the pleas of the American people for immigration enforcement and border security. By finally enforcing our immigration laws, we will raise wages, help the unemployed, save billions and billions of dollars, and make our communities safer for everyone. We want all Americans to succeed, but that can't happen in an environment of lawless chaos. We must restore integrity and the rule of law at our borders.

For that reason, we will soon begin the construction of a great, great wall along our southern border. As we speak tonight, we are removing gang members, drug dealers, and criminals that threaten our communities and prey on our very innocent citizens. Bad ones are going out as I speak, and as I promised throughout the campaign.

To any in Congress who do not believe we should enforce our laws, I would ask you this one question: What would you say to the American family that loses their jobs, their income, or their loved one because America refused to uphold its laws and defends its borders?

Our obligation is to serve, protect, and defend the citizens of the United States. We are also taking strong measures to protect our nation from radical Islamic terrorism. According to data provided by the Department of Justice, the vast majority of individuals convicted of terrorism and terrorism-related offenses since 9/11 came here from outside of our country. We have seen the attacks at home - - from Boston to San Bernardino to the Pentagon, and, yes, even the World Trade Center.

We have seen the attacks in France, in Belgium, in Germany, and all over the world. It is not compassionate, but reckless to allow uncontrolled entry from places where proper vetting cannot occur. Those given the high honor of admission to the United States should support this country and love its people and its values. We cannot allow a beachhead of terrorism to form inside America. We cannot allow our nation to become a sanctuary for extremists.

That is why my administration has been working on improved vetting procedures, and we will shortly take new steps to keep our nation safe and to keep out those out who will do us harm.

As promised, I directed the Department of Defense to develop a plan to demolish and destroy ISIS -- a network of lawless savages that have slaughtered Muslims and Christians, and men, and women, and children of all faiths and all beliefs. We will work with our allies, including our friends and allies in the Muslim world, to extinguish this vile enemy from our planet.

I have also imposed new sanctions on entities and individuals who support Iran's ballistic missile program, and reaffirmed our unbreakable alliance with the State of Israel.

Finally, I have kept my promise to appoint a justice to the United States Supreme Court, from my list of 20 judges, who will defend our Constitution.

I am greatly honored to have Maureen Scalia with us in the gallery tonight. Thank you, Maureen. Her late, great husband, Antonin Scalia, will forever be a symbol of American justice. To fill his seat, we have chosen Judge Neil Gorsuch, a man of incredible skill and deep devotion to the law. He was confirmed unanimously by the Court of Appeals, and I am asking the Senate to swiftly approve his nomination.

Tonight, as I outline the next steps we must take as a country, we must honestly acknowledge the circumstances we inherited. Ninety-four million Americans are out of the labor force. Over 43 million people are now living in poverty, and over 43 million Americans are on food stamps. More than one in five people in their prime working years are not working. We have the worst financial recovery in 65 years. In the last eight years, the past administration has put on more new debt than nearly all of the other Presidents combined.

We've lost more than one-fourth of our manufacturing jobs since NAFTA was approved, and we've lost 60,000 factories since China joined the World Trade Organization in 2001. Our trade deficit in goods with the world last year was nearly $800 billion dollars. And overseas we have inherited a series of tragic foreign policy disasters.

Solving these and so many other pressing problems will require us to work past the differences of party. It will require us to tap into the American spirit that has overcome every challenge throughout our long and storied history. But to accomplish our goals at home and abroad, we must restart the engine of the American economy -- making it easier for companies to do business in the United States, and much, much harder for companies to leave our country.

Right now, American companies are taxed at one of the highest rates anywhere in the world. My economic team is developing historic tax reform that will reduce the tax rate on our companies so they can compete and thrive anywhere and with anyone. It will be a big, big cut.

At the same time, we will provide massive tax relief for the middle class. We must create a level playing field for American companies and our workers. We have to do it. Currently, when we ship products out of America, many other countries make us pay very high tariffs and taxes. But when foreign companies ship their products into America, we charge them nothing, or almost nothing.

I just met with officials and workers from a great American company, Harley-Davidson. In fact, they proudly displayed five of their magnificent motorcycles, made in the USA, on the front lawn of the White House. ((Laughter and applause.) And they wanted me to ride one and I said, "No, thank you." (Laughter.)

At our meeting, I asked them, how are you doing, how is business? They said that it's good. I asked them further, how are you doing with other countries, mainly international sales? They told me -- without even complaining, because they have been so mistreated for so long that they've become used to it -- that it's very hard to do business with other countries because they tax our goods at such a high rate. They said that in the case of another country, they taxed their motorcycles at 100 percent. They weren't even asking for a change. But I am.

I believe strongly in free trade but it also has to be fair trade. It's been a long time since we had fair trade. The first Republican President, Abraham Lincoln, warned that the "abandonment of the protective policy by the American government... will produce want and ruin among our people." Lincoln was right -- and it's time we heeded his advice and his words. I am not going to let America and its great companies and workers be taken advantage of us any longer. They have taken advantage of our country. No longer.

I am going to bring back millions of jobs. Protecting our workers also means reforming our system of legal immigration. The current, outdated system depresses wages for our poorest workers, and puts great pressure on taxpayers. Nations around the world, like Canada, Australia and many others, have a merit-based immigration system. It's a basic principle that those seeking to enter a country ought to be able to support themselves financially. Yet, in America, we do not enforce this rule, straining the very public resources that our poorest citizens rely upon. According to the National Academy of Sciences, our current immigration system costs American taxpayers many billions of dollars a year.

Switching away from this current system of lower-skilled immigration, and instead adopting a merit-based system, we will have so many more benefits. It will save countless dollars, raise workers' wages, and help struggling families -- including immigrant families -- enter the middle class. And they will do it quickly, and they will be very, very happy, indeed.

I believe that real and positive immigration reform is possible, as long as we focus on the following goals: To improve jobs and wages for Americans; to strengthen our nation's security; and to restore respect for our laws. If we are guided by the wellbeing of American citizens, then I believe Republicans and Democrats can work together to achieve an outcome that has eluded our country for decades.

Another Republican President, Dwight D. Eisenhower, initiated the last truly great national infrastructure program - - the building of the Interstate Highway System. The time has come for a new program of national rebuilding.

America has spent approximately $6 trillion in the Middle East -- all the while our infrastructure at home is crumbling. With this $6 trillion, we could have rebuilt our country twice, and maybe even three times if we had people who had the ability to negotiate.

To launch our national rebuilding, I will be asking Congress to approve legislation that produces a $1 trillion investment in infrastructure of the United States -- financed through both public and private capital -- creating millions of new jobs. This effort will be guided by two core principles: buy American and hire American.

Tonight, I am also calling on this Congress to repeal and replace "Obamacare" with reforms that expand choice, increase access, lower costs, and, at the same time, provide better healthcare.

Mandating every American to buy government-approved health insurance was never the right solution for our country. The way to make health insurance available to everyone is to lower the cost of health insurance, and that is what we are going to do.

"Obamacare" premiums nationwide have increased by double and triple digits. As an example, Arizona went up 116 percent last year alone. Governor Matt Bevin of Kentucky just said "Obamacare" is failing in his state -- the state of Kentucky -- and it's unsustainable and collapsing.

One-third of counties have only one insurer, and they are losing them fast. They are losing them so fast. They are leaving, and many Americans have no choice at all. There's no choice left. Remember when you were told that you could keep your doctor and keep your plan? We now know that all of those promises have been totally broken. "Obamacare" is collapsing, and we must act decisively to protect all Americans.

Action is not a choice, it is a necessity. So, I am calling on all Democrats and Republicans in Congress to work with us to save Americans from this imploding "Obamacare" disaster.

Here are the principles that should guide the Congress as we move to create a better healthcare system for all Americans:

First, we should ensure that Americans with preexisting conditions have access to coverage, and that we have a stable transition for Americans currently enrolled in the healthcare exchanges.

Secondly, we should help Americans purchase their own coverage through the use of tax credits and expanded Health Savings Accounts -- but it must be the plan they want, not the plan forced on them by our government.

Thirdly, we should give our great state governors the resources and flexibility they need with Medicaid to make sure no one is left out.

Fourth, we should implement legal reforms that protect patients and doctors from unnecessary costs that drive up the price of insurance, and work to bring down the artificially high price of drugs, and bring them down immediately.

And finally, the time has come to give Americans the freedom to purchase health insurance across state lines which will create a truly competitive national marketplace that will bring costs way down and provide far better care. So important.

Everything that is broken in our country can be fixed. Every problem can be solved. And every hurting family can find healing and hope.

Our citizens deserve this, and so much more -- so why not join forces and finally get the job done, and get it done right? On this and so many other things, Democrats and Republicans should get together and unite for the good of our country and for the good of the American people.

My administration wants to work with members of both parties to make childcare accessible and affordable, to help ensure new parents that they have paid family leave to invest in women's health, and to promote clean air and clean water, and to rebuild our military and our infrastructure.

True love for our people requires us to find common ground, to advance the common good, and to cooperate on behalf of every American child who deserves a much brighter future.

An incredible young woman is with us this evening, who should serve as an inspiration to us all. Today is Rare Disease Day, and joining us in the gallery is a rare disease survivor, Megan Crowley.

Megan was diagnosed with Pompe disease, a rare and serious illness, when she was 15 months old. She was not expected to live past five. On receiving this news, Megan's dad, John, fought with everything he had to save the life of his precious child. He founded a company to look for a cure, and helped develop the drug that saved Megan's life.

Today she is 20 years old and a sophomore at Notre Dame.

Megan's story is about the unbounded power of a father's love for a daughter. But our slow and burdensome approval process at the Food and Drug Administration keeps too many advances, like the one that saved Megan's life, from reaching those in need. If we slash the restraints, not just at the FDA but across our government, then we will be blessed with far more miracles just like Megan. In fact, our children will grow up in a nation of miracles.

But to achieve this future, we must enrich the mind and the souls of every American child. Education is the civil rights issue of our time. I am calling upon members of both parties to pass an education bill that funds school choice for disadvantaged youth, including millions of African American and Latino children. These families should be free to choose the public, private, charter, magnet, religious, or home school that is right for them.

Joining us tonight in the gallery is a remarkable woman, Denisha Merriweather. As a young girl, Denisha struggled in school and failed third grade twice. But then she was able to enroll in a private center for learning -- a great learning center -- with the help of a tax credit and a scholarship program.

Today, she is the first in her family to graduate, not just from high school, but from college. Later this year she will get her master's degree in social work. We want all children to be able to break the cycle of poverty just like Denisha.

But to break the cycle of poverty, we must also break the cycle of violence. The murder rate in 2015 experienced its largest single-year increase in nearly half a century. In Chicago, more than 4,000 people were shot last year alone, and the murder rate so far this year has been even higher. This is not acceptable in our society.

Every American child should be able to grow up in a safe community, to attend a great school, and to have access to a high-paying job. But to create this future, we must work with, not against -- not against -- the men and women of law enforcement. We must build bridges of cooperation and trust -- not drive the wedge of disunity and, really, it's what it is, division. It's pure, unadulterated division. We have to unify.

Police and sheriffs are members of our community. They're friends and neighbors, they're mothers and fathers, sons and daughters -- and they leave behind loved ones every day who worry about whether or not they'll come home safe and sound. We must support the incredible men and women of law enforcement.

And we must support the victims of crime. I have ordered the Department of Homeland Security to create an office to serve American victims. The office is called VOICE -- Victims of Immigration Crime Engagement. We are providing a voice to those who have been ignored by our media and silenced by special interests. Joining us in the audience tonight are four very brave Americans whose government failed them. Their names are Jamiel Shaw, Susan Oliver, Jenna Oliver, and Jessica Davis.

Jamiel's 17-year-old son was viciously murdered by an illegal immigrant gang member who had just been released from prison. Jamiel Shaw, Jr. was an incredible young man, with unlimited potential who was getting ready to go to college where he would have excelled as a great college quarterback. But he never got the chance. His father, who is in the audience tonight, has become a very good friend of mine. Jamiel, thank you. Thank you.

Also with us are Susan Oliver and Jessica Davis. Their husbands, Deputy Sheriff Danny Oliver and Detective Michael Davis, were slain in the line of duty in California. They were pillars of their community. These brave men were viciously gunned down by an illegal immigrant with a criminal record and two prior deportations. Should have never been in our country.

Sitting with Susan is her daughter, Jenna. Jenna, I want you to know that your father was a hero, and that tonight you have the love of an entire country supporting you and praying for you.

To Jamiel, Jenna, Susan and Jessica, I want you to know that we will never stop fighting for justice. Your loved ones will never, ever be forgotten. We will always honor their memory.

Finally, to keep America safe, we must provide the men and women of the United States military with the tools they need to prevent war -- if they must -- they have to fight and they only have to win.

I am sending Congress a budget that rebuilds the military, eliminates the defense sequester and calls for one of the largest increases in national defense spending in American history. My budget will also increase funding for our veterans. Our veterans have delivered for this nation, and now we must deliver for them.

The challenges we face as a nation are great, but our people are even greater. And none are greater or braver than those who fight for America in uniform.

We are blessed to be joined tonight by Carryn Owens, the widow of a U.S. Navy Special Operator, Senior Chief William "Ryan" Owens. Ryan died as he lived: a warrior and a hero, battling against terrorism and securing our nation. I just spoke to our great General Mattis, just now, who reconfirmed that -- and I quote -- "Ryan was a part of a highly successful raid that generated large amounts of vital intelligence that will lead to many more victories in the future against our enemies." Ryan's legacy is etched into eternity. Thank you. And Ryan is looking down, right now --

you know that -- and he is very happy because I think he just broke a record. (Laughter and applause.)

For as the Bible teaches us, "There is no greater act of love than to lay down one's life for one's friends." Ryan laid down his life for his friends, for his country, and for our freedom. And we will never forget Ryan.

To those allies who wonder what kind of a friend America will be, look no further than the heroes who wear our uniform. Our foreign policy calls for a direct, robust and meaningful engagement with the world. It is American leadership based on vital security interests that we share with our allies all across the globe.

We strongly support NATO, an alliance forged through the bonds of two world wars that dethroned fascism, and a Cold War, and defeated communism.

But our partners must meet their financial obligations. And now, based on our very strong and frank discussions, they are beginning to do just that. In fact, I can tell you, the money is pouring in. Very nice. We expect our partners -- whether in NATO, the Middle East, or in the Pacific -- to take a direct and meaningful role in both strategic and military operations, and pay their fair share of the cost. Have to do that.

We will respect historic institutions, but we will respect the foreign rights of all nations, and they have to respect our rights as a nation also. Free nations are the best vehicle for expressing the will of the people, and America respects the right of all nations to chart their own path. My job is not to represent the world. My job is to represent the United States of America.

But we know that America is better off when there is less conflict, not more. We must learn from the mistakes of the past. We have seen the war and the destruction that have ravaged and raged throughout the world -- all across the world. The only long-term solution for these humanitarian disasters, in many cases, is to create the conditions where displaced persons can safely return home and begin the long, long process of rebuilding.

America is willing to find new friends, and to forge new partnerships, where shared interests align. We want harmony and stability, not war and conflict. We want peace, wherever peace can be found.

America is friends today with former enemies. Some of our closest allies, decades ago, fought on the opposite side of these terrible, terrible wars. This history should give us all faith in the possibilities for a better world. Hopefully, the 250th year for America will see a world that is more peaceful, more just, and more free.

On our 100th anniversary, in 1876, citizens from across our nation came to Philadelphia to celebrate America's centennial. At that celebration, the country's builders and artists and inventors showed off their wonderful creations.

Alexander Graham Bell displayed his telephone for the first time. Remington unveiled the first typewriter. An early attempt was made at electric light. Thomas Edison showed an automatic telegraph and an electric pen. Imagine the wonders our country could know in America's 250th year.

Think of the marvels we can achieve if we simply set free the dreams of our people. Cures to the illnesses that have always plagued us are not too much to hope. American footprints on distant worlds are not too big a dream. Millions lifted from welfare to work is not too much to expect. And streets where mothers are safe from fear, schools where children learn in peace, and jobs where Americans prosper and grow are not too much to ask.

When we have all of this, we will have made America greater than ever before -- for all Americans. This is our vision. This is our mission. But we can only get there together. We are one people, with one destiny. We all bleed the same blood. We all salute the same great American flag. And we all are made by the same God.

When we fulfill this vision, when we celebrate our 250 years of glorious freedom, we will look back on tonight as when this new chapter of American Greatness began. The time for small thinking is over. The time for trivial fights is behind us. We just need the courage to share the dreams that fill our hearts, the bravery to express the hopes that stir our souls, and the confidence to turn those hopes and those dreams into action.

From now on, America will be empowered by our aspirations, not burdened by our fears; inspired by the future, not bound by the failures of the past; and guided by our vision, not blinded by our doubts.

I am asking all citizens to embrace this renewal of the American spirit. I am asking all members of Congress to join me in dreaming big, and bold, and daring things for our country. I am asking everyone watching tonight to seize this moment. Believe in yourselves, believe in your future, and believe, once more, in America.

Thank you, God bless you, and God bless the United States.

END

An analysis of the speech made by Donald Trump to the joint sessions reveals that the president added more flesh to the promises he made during his campaign. In a nutshell, he reiterated his promise to:

- carry out fundamental economic changes to the American economy, including reforms in taxation, international trade, and free trade, and pursue a policy of America first that smacks of economic nationalism
- reform immigration by focusing more on lowering low-skilled immigration to the USA, careful vetting, border enforcement, and immigration that serves the

interests of the United States of America and Americans

- carry out fundamental healthcare reforms which entail the repealing and replacement of "Obamacare" with something "better"
- Bring about reforms that would empower America's schoolchildren through a School Choice Agenda that entails exploring education savings accounts for military-connected children, expanding education choice options for families by making it possible for K–12 education costs to be classified as allowable expenditures under 529 plans for college savings, the establishment of education savings accounts for children attending Bureau of Indian Education schools, reauthorizing the District of Columbia (D.C) Opportunity Scholarship Program, and the expansion of choice in the District of Columbia to make the entire area student-centered and portable.
- Upgrade the US military, maintain America's leadership in NATO, and make other NATO members live up to their obligations to the military organization.
- Tap both private and public sources to carry out a $1 trillion "new program of national rebuilding" that would upgrade the standard of the infrastructure in the USA by making the fixing of the country's roads, bridges, tunnels, airports, and railways that are falling apart a major priority of his administration.
- Improve law and order in the country.

"What a speech!"

That exclamation and similar ones were echoed by individuals from different quarters. Even some of Donald Trump's virulent opponents voiced words of praise along those lines in reaction to his above speech. It was apparent to all that the 45th president of the United States of America cut across the board of America's political spectrum with his 2017 formal address to the joint sessions. In fact, CNN's Van Jones who had been extremely critical of the president praised him for honoring the widow of a Navy SEAL killed during a raid in Yemen among other things with the following words, *"he became president of the United States at that moment, period...There are a lot of people who have a lot of reasons to be frustrated with him, to be fearful of him, to be mad at him, but that was one of the most extraordinary moments you have ever seen in American politics, period."*

Donald Trump's subsequent addresses were along similar lines. However, over the next two years, Americans found themselves subjected to developments arising from wrangling between its different political classes and factions that went a long way to prove that the message of reconciliation and exhortation in that speech asking all Americans to join hands and take the country to greater heights fell flat. Bi-partisan rivalry never left the center stage of American politics and it does not look like it would recede into the shadows any time soon.

Subsequent chapters and part two of the book shall elaborate on this subject and the outcome of the Trump presidency. They shall be determined by how Donald Trump and his administration live up to the speech he made in the joint sessions that day, and by how the forces arrayed against him work with or against him. Whatever that outcome turns out to be, it is certainly going to be colorful indeed for some people.

CHAPTER FIVE

Balance Sheet on Promises

"There are no secrets to success. It is the result of preparation, hard work, and learning from failure."
Colin Powell

Americans and the rest of the world are counting thirty months into the Trump presidency; so it would be foolhardy to ask them if they think Donald Trump is going to renege on his promises, work with the Congress, the Bureaucracy and the Judiciary in carrying out piecemeal reforms to move the country forward without threatening the fabrics of the state and the United States of America's unique position in the world, as most of those who doubted him back in January 2017 thought he was going to do.

Most Trump supporters are convinced that their president is on track to score an A+ in fulfilling the promises he made before he won the presidency. After all, they voted for him on the premise that he would challenge the political establishment and change things in a manner that would benefit the common man in America as well as those who are in the country legally. These "Trumpists" are mostly people who considered the system to be rigged and designed to be advantageous only to a fraction of the population of the country. They actually thought the system had been ripping them off over the years.

We only have to go back to Michael Moore, the neoliberal American documentary filmmaker and author, to his very revealing statements about Donald Trump and the people rooting for him when he said the following just before the 2016 presidential election:

> "People are upset. They're angry at the system and they see Trump—not so much that they agree with him—but they see him as the human Molotov cocktail that they get to toss into the system with Brexit and blow it up, send a message..."

A pundit who downplays the importance of that point of view, and then proceeds to explain how the Trump presidency would pan out in the next months and years, would be judged to be no better than a novice expecting to get out of an extensive labyrinth without a compass or a roadmap. That in a way also explains the nuanced political figure that the current president is. So it is not surprising to find a good number of experts in the field of American politics that are comfortable stating that Donald Trump's position has shifted to the point where his current political ideology is now a cross between democracy, capitalism, and socialism. That view, of course, is contrary to what is held by most analysts, especially those in the mainstream who are convinced that nothing fundamental has changed about Donald Trump over the years. Michael Moore could have been echoing the legendary American television and radio host Larry King when he succinctly expressed the point of view of the last group by saying that:

> *"His ideology is called Donald J. Trump. He believes in Donald J. Trump. If it's good for him, then it's a good thing. Not good for him, it's a bad thing..."*

However, for those who have put the 45th president on a pedestal, and even for those who had no preconceptions about him and so try to make sense of his actions and policies in an unbiased manner, it is difficult to see any truth in the above perceptions, especially after the president's 2017 speech to the joint sessions. That speech alone made it difficult for an optimistic person to take Trump critics seriously, even if the critic happened to be someone of renown like Professor Noam Chomsky who is considered by many as the greatest intellectual alive.

The great American historian, linguist, philosopher, political activist, cognitive scientist, and social critic whose mastery of analytic philosophy is enviable had good reasons to say that *"The people behind Trump have a systematic and consistent plan to enrich the wealthy and hurt the poor..."* Respectable though the statement is,

Professor Chomsky's position defied the spirit of that speech made by Donald Trump, irrespective of the fact that his view was based on plausibility, supported by the fact that most of the people Donald Trump picked to head the top positions in his administration are from the corporate world, the financial establishment and from big business. To make the point, we only have to take the case of Rex Tillerson, the first Secretary of State in the Trump administration, who before his appointment was the chief executive officer of ExxonMobil.

Even views by Trump critics that he is a threat to world peace, and that he poses a major danger to humanity as a whole for pulling the plug on the support the United States was giving to the world effort to combat climate change among other things, are now taken less seriously than before because many of these same critics are accused of taking a belligerent stand on the issue of projecting or protecting American military, economic and political power abroad, thereby putting the world at risk of trade wars, further military conflicts, and even a nuclear war.

When we take into account the fact that these developments are taking place at a time that an unusually high proportion of the world's renowned analysts, intellectuals, and even eschatologist of the different Abrahamic religions believe that we are on the eve of the endpoint or end time—a period full of turmoil epitomized by current problems such as the deluge of refugees, threats of new catastrophes, explosion of racism and supremacism around the world, particularly in places like the USA and Europe—the quest for a leading figure with the steel nerves and the commitment to knock some sense into the heads of those who have been carrying out their solipsistic agendas of world domination, ceases being an urgent need and becomes an imperative. And like it or not, some 35% of the American electorate that have formed the solid base of Trump supporters and militants see in the 45th president of the United States of America that person with the steel nerves or that Michael Moore's "Molotov Cocktail" that would blast away most of the injustices emanating from a political system that has been partially infiltrated by interest groups. That begs the question:

How committed is the supposedly steel-nerved Donald Trump in fixing the system that has regulated the socio-economic and political life of the United States of American since its founding almost two and a half-century ago?

We only need to take a look at Donald Trump's core promises, which were analyzed in the previous chapters, and then shore them up with other important promises like the ones below to get an idea of his overall performance. What then comes up is the scorecard that leaves room for optimism on America's future domestic and foreign performance, especially if Donald Trump and his administration manage to make effective use of the remaining months of his first term in office by rising above the fray that characterizes bipartisan politics in the United States of America and by scoring big on improving the lot of the majority of the American people.

A Table of Donald Trump's Crucial Pre-Election Promises

	PROMISES	BEING WORKED ON	STALLED	NOT YET RATED	KEPT	COMPROMISED	BROKEN
1	Impose the death penalty for cop killers		X				
2	Defund Planned Parenthood		X				
3	No Cuts to Medicare				X		
4	No Cuts to Medicaid		X				
5	Reverse Obama's 2016- gun executive order				X		
6	Reform mental health programs and institutions.	X					
7	Expand mental health programs	X					
8	Make concealed carry permit (right to carry) valid in all 50 states	X					
9	Appoint a special prosecutor to investigate Hillary Clinton		X				
10	Open up libel laws		X				
11	Restrict internet use by ISIS		X				
12	Plan to defeat ISIS	X					
13	Champion an international		X				

conference to defeat ISIS

#		Col A	Col B	Col C	Col D
14	Move U.S. Embassy to Jerusalem			X	
15	Cancel job-killing regulation and put a moratorium on new ones.	X			
16	Keep Guantanamo Bay Detention Center open			X	
17	Establish a commission on radical Islam				X
18	Ensure funding for historic black colleges	X			
19	Bring back (Restore) manufacturing	X			
20	Increase the size of the U.S. Army to 540,000 active-duty soldiers	X			
21	Rebuild the Marine Corps from 23 to 36 battalions	X			
22	Rebuild an Air Force of at least 1,200 fighter aircraft	X			
23	Build a Navy of 350 surface ships and submarines.	X			
24	Cancel visas to countries that refuse to take back undocumented immigrants	X			
25	Defund Planned Parenthood	X			
26	A $20 billion Increase to federal investment toward School Choice		X		
27	Create a 24 hour a day private White House hotline for veterans			X	
28	Cancel the Paris Climate Agreement			X	

#	Item				
29	Cancel Climate Change payments to the United Nations			X	
30	Guarantee 6-week paid leave	X			
31	Require price transparency from health care providers		X		
32	Allow individuals to use Health Savings Accounts (HSAs).		X		
33	Pass legislation to allow health insurance across state lines	X			
34	Administer Medicaid through block grants		X		
35	Allow individuals to fully deduct health insurance premium payments from their tax returns				X
36	Allow free access to the drug market	X			
37	Release his tax returns after an audit is completed				X
38	Sue those who accused him of sexual misconduct				X
39	Use American steel for American infrastructure.		X		
40	Increase visa fees		X		
41	Declare China a currency manipulator				X
42	Repatriate existing Syrian refugees				X
43	Make it a nationwide policy to hire Americans first.	X			
44	Make a minimum		X		

sentence mandatory for criminals caught trying to enter the United States illegally.

#	Item					
45	Increase the economic growth rate to 4% annually	X				
46	Get rid of the $19 trillion federal debt in 8 years	X				
47	End birthright citizenship		X			
48	Would not take vacations	X				
49	Resume the "Merry Christmas" instead of the recent "Happy Holidays"			X		
50	Ban on foreign lobbyists raising money for American elections		X			
51	Replace J-1 Visa with Inner City Resume Bank			X		
52	Dramatically scale the Department of Education.	X				
53	Eliminate the estate or death tax				X	
54	Create a 10-percent repatriation tax	X		X		
55	A quick and fair balance of the federal budget					X
56	Cut taxes for everyone				X	
57	Dramatically scale back the EPA (Environmental Protection Agency)	X				
58	Triple ICE (Immigration and Customs Enforcement)				X	
59	Revive the coal industry	X				
60	End birthright citizenship		X			
61	Stop the AT&T Time					X

	Warner Merger					
62	Eliminate gun-free zones at school and military bases	X				
63	Reverse China's entry into the World Trade Organization					X
64	Withdraw from Trans-Pacific Partnership			X		
65	Eliminate wasteful spending in every department	X				
66	Suspend immigration from terror-prone places			X		
67	Deport criminal undocumented immigrants	X				
68	Deport all undocumented immigrants	X				
69	Save the Carrier plant in Indiana				X	
70	Space out the scheduling of vaccinations for children		X			
71	Reduce Federal Spending (Penny Plan) over 10 years		X			

- KEPT: Donald Trump delivered on the promise(s) he made.

- COMPROMISED: Donald Trump did not accomplish every part of his original goal, due to compromises made on certain details to get the things done.

- BROKEN: The president failed to accomplish his stated objective.

- BEING WORKED ON: Donald Trump has taken steps toward fulfilling the promise or goal but is yet to complete it.

- STALLED: Donald Trump has not taken significant action(s) to fulfill this promise.

- NOT YET RATED: Promise yet to be rated either because no action has been taken to fulfill it or because it is unattainable.

The above scorecard bodes well with Donald Trump's ambition to leave the White House at the end of his term(s) as an accomplished president. In fact, Politico, the Arlington, Virginia-based American political journalism company that covers politics and policy in the United States and abroad, appears to go in line with the analysis done so far, based on the light it shed on the president's performance vis-a-vis his promises. The table below indicates that:

May 2019 Trump-O-Meter Scorecard by Politico

	NUMBERS	PERCENTAGE (%)
PROMISES		
Being Worked On	28	27.5
Stalled	28	27.5
Kept	18	16.7
Compromised	11	10.8
Broken	18	17.6

Most pundits give 174 as the figure or number of promises Donald Trump made to the electorate before he became the 45th president of the United States of America. The above scorecard is a tally of the promises he addressed in one way or the other. So, it is logical to say that he has grappled with 65% of the promises he made during 63% of his term in office.

CHAPTER SIX

The Salamander

"The opposite of love is not hate, it's indifference. The opposite of art is not ugliness, it's indifference. The opposite of faith is not heresy, it's indifference. And the opposite of life is not death, it's indifference."

Elie Wiesel

"Trust is earned, respect is given, and loyalty is demonstrated. Betrayal of any one of those is to lose all three."

Ziad K. Abdelnour

"A nationalist will blindly follow his country to his death out of love for it. A patriot will stand up for and even against his country to his death out of love for it."

Janvier Chouteu-Chando

People, and more especially the category of Americans whose loyalty to anyone or to any entity hinges on the personal benefits they derive from having a relationship with that person or body, have a hard time understanding the nature of Donald Trump's support base. The disconnect can be traced way back, even before the start of his presidency, when many pundits and analysts of different shades first tried to elaborate on the rationale for the 35 percent solid support that the president had been commanding among the electorate since his election into the Oval Office, as if everything depends on empirical formulas. However, the past two and a half years have exposed several flaws in the analysis postulated by some of these gurus or savants on the nature of Donald Trump's core supporters.

How does one then explain the fact that the Republican Party which traditionally catered for the interest of the wealthy class and which drew much of its support from the country's deeply religious, is having a billionaire Republican in the White House who nevertheless commands the support of a medley range of Americans that Hillary Clinton described as a "Basket of Deplorables", the majority of whom are economically underprivileged, yet constitute the group that has the highest percentage of his core supporters?

The fact that this category of Americans rose from 35 percent in early 2017 to 36 percent in April 2019, with the increase coming from all the racial groups in the country, presents an intriguing angle for any gung-ho analysts.

We don't have to think deeply or look far to figure out

why many people find that increase among Donald Trump's core supporters intriguing. The anticipation that accompanied the 2018-2019 shutdown when most of his opponents and even some of those who were not really against him thought that the standoff between Republicans and Democrats in Congress over funding for the president's proposed border wall would shrink the size of his core supporters, was grounded on solid analysis. However, the opposition's expectations of political gains from that hiccup turned out to be a pyrrhic victory only. All the different polls taken since January 2019 show a consistent drop in the percentage of Americans who disapprove of Donald Trump's presidency, a decline that has been steady to the point where the president's core support base has risen to 36 percent of adult Americans.

Trump Administration's 2019 Approval Rating

Company/Monthly Percentages	January 2019	February 2019	March 2019	April 2019	May 2019
Ipsos (for Reuters)	39%	41%	42%	39%	39%
YouGov (for The Economist)	37%	40%	43%	42%	42%
Investor's Business Daily	42%	39%	41%	41%	43%
NBC News/Wall Street Journal	43%	46%	53%		46%
Gallup	37%	43%	39%	46%	

There are certain things, certain people and certain situations that the well-informed mind has a hard time fathoming. Donald Trump happens to be one of them. So much dirt has been flung at him that his approval ratings should have plummeted to the point where we should be expecting him to suffer a humiliating loss in the 2020 presidential election with a lower percentage or vote count than even Jimmy Carter, who as an incumbent, lost the 1984 Presidential Election by 41% (35,480,115) to Ronald Reagan's 50.7% (43,903,230). It is as if the American people, or more specifically Donald Trump's core supporters, have come to the conclusion that American politics, like that of many other countries dominated by powerful interest groups, is replete with intrigues, conspiracies, make-beliefs, and secret plans; it is as if they are seeing something of Machiavelli in those opposing the 45th president and so are reacting to it instinctively and calculatingly by distrusting the mainstream media that harps on allegations, many of which are baseless, that the president colluded with Russia, obstructed justice, etc.

Donald Trump's core supporters distrust the bureaucracy made up of cabinet departments, government corporations, independent agencies, and regulatory commissions; they wonder about the bureaucracy that sees the United States of America as the world's only military, economic and diplomatic superpower and seems determined to do whatever it takes to continue leading the world. The corporate media and the bureaucracy have become less attractive to the majority of these Trump core supporters since he started regulating American affairs from the Oval Office.

It would be wrong to say that there is no truth in all the accusations that have been made against the 45th US. president, or that he does not deserve all the dirt that has been thrown at him. The United States of America's first gentleman has an abrasive personality among other things, which is why it would surprise nobody that he has irked some of the people he crossed paths with. And based on a scorecard of scandals and allegations against him, it is easy to conclude that he is attracted to actions that many consider morally wrong and borderline legal, while having strong immunity against them at the same time. I say so because Donald Trump has put up an ambivalent defense to the accusations heaped on him by his opponents calling to question his pledge to "Drain the Swamp" in Washington DC, yet he seems unscathed by these charges or claims.

If not:

- then how can one explain the failure to provide damaging information or the sudden quietness about the entanglements involving Donald Trump's family, his businesses and his presidency, especially the much-talked-about Trump Organization which he has not divested from, a lucrative business per se that generated at least $500 million in revenue in 2017 and $479 million in 2018?

- what is the explanation for the fizzling out of the

defamation lawsuit by 15 women who claimed he sexually assaulted them?

- how does one explain the crumbling of the allegation by the former porn star Stormy Daniels (real name Stephanie Clifford) that she had an affair with the then president-to-be in 2006 and that Donald Trump's lawyer Michael Cohen paid her the sum of $130,000 to be quiet about it ahead of the 2016 presidential election, an action that is considered a campaign finance violation, and which is one of the eight federal crimes that Michael Cohen confessed to and is serving a three-year prison term for?

- what do we give as an explanation for the bungling nature of his staff or political retinue involving such scandals as the spending of hundreds of thousands of dollars on private planes by the former secretary of Health and Human Services Tom Price; the Housing and Urban Development Secretary Ben Carson's indiscretion in allowing his son to help organize an agency listening tour in Baltimore even though he had been warned against it by government lawyers on grounds that it would violate ethics rules?

- how come nothing came out of the claims of sexual assault made by three women against Brett Michael Kavanaugh whom the 45th president of the United

States of America nominated to replace Anthony McLeod Kennedy, the 93rd Associate Justice of the Supreme Court of the United States who served from 1988 until his retirement in 2018 Et cetera?

The above amputations, of course, stand out as a pale shadow of the list of accusations against the 45th president that have proven to be of no consequence. However, that does not mean the president and his retinue are unscathed.

The story of Russian hacking and Russia influencing the 2016 US. presidential election, and the belief that Donald Trump or some members of his team worked with the Russians and other foreign entities to help him win the presidency has clouded the American president's everyday activities for sure. It is as if nothing would assuage the situation for the president; not even the claims by the Russian president Vladimir Putin that there was no Russian involvement in the election, when he stated among other things that *"The hysteria is merely caused by the fact that somebody needs to divert the attention of the American people from the essence of what was exposed by the hackers."*

Many Americans, mostly supporters of Donald Trump think the Russian president is right. They too see a conspiracy by the mainstream media and the Democratic Party to divert attention away from themselves and disarray the Trump presidency and its original intention to cultivate good relations between Russia and the United States of America.